HOLY
COW!

HOLY COW!

BY

HARRY CARAY

with

BOB VERDI

VILLARD BOOKS / NEW YORK / 1989

Library of Congress Cataloging-in-Publication Data

Caray, Harry.
  Holy cow!

  1. Caray, Harry.   2. Sportscasters—United States—
Biography.   I. Verdi, Bob.   II. Title.
GV742.42.C37A3   1989   070.4′49796′0924 [B]   85-40859
ISBN 0-394-55103-6

Design by Robert Bull Design

Manufactured in the United States of America

9 8 7 6 5 4 3 2

First Edition

This book is dedicated to Doxie Argint, who, as an aunt, was the closest thing I ever had to a mother.

And a special dedication to those who have had the biggest impact on my career, the most important but least appreciated force in all sports—the fans. Without them, nobody, including me, could have accomplished much at all. My greatest professional incentive has been to try to please them. So this book is for them, with profound appreciation for their long friendship.

HOLY COW!

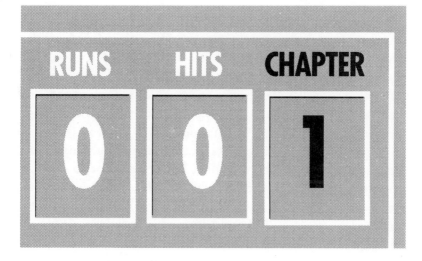

"GLAD TO BE ALIVE"

FEBRUARY 17, 1986–It started out as a routine day for me, but it certainly didn't wind up that way.

I woke up at midmorning in our winter home in Palm Springs, California, and felt great. Every morning, my routine is the same. I walk to the store to buy the newspapers—the two from Los Angeles, the *Times* and *Herald-Examiner,* plus *USA Today.* In the afternoon, when the first airplane arrives from Chicago, I get the *Chicago Tribune* and *Chicago Sun-Times,* too. Fritzie Gauna, a friend of ours who keeps an eye on the house when we're back in Chicago during the summer, goes to the Palm Springs Airport and picks up the two Chicago papers. You have to keep up with world events, you know.

Anyway, it's about a three-mile round trip for me to the store and then back to the house. When I returned home that day,

I rode my stationary bike for about seven miles, then did some exercises for my back, and went in the Jacuzzi for a little while. By the time I took care of that ritual, and read a little, it was time to head over to the Canyon Country Club, just down the road. Sometimes I walk. We're right on the sixth fairway of the golf course, so it's not much of a walk. About twelve holes long. Sometimes I walk. On this particular day, I drove over.

It was about four-thirty in the afternoon, past Budweiser time and headed toward happy hour. I went to the bar to order a scotch old-fashioned when one of the fellows nearby said another guy was needed in a gin game. I gladly joined in, and to make a long story short, I was doing pretty well. I was up about five hundred dollars when I suddenly realized I was having trouble picking up the cards with my right hand. I had no pain, and I didn't feel dizzy, and I must have been pretty alert. As I said, I was up about five hundred dollars.

I got up from the table and went into the bathroom and threw some cold water on my face. Again, I felt no pain. Then I went back to the card game and lost a hand. At that point, Mel Green, a friend of mine, looked over and said, "You better stop, Harry. You should go on home right away."

To my knowledge, I was talking all right and acting all right, but the other people there must have sized up that something was wrong. As I said, I drove to the club that day, but Mel wasn't about to let me take the car back home. He drove me, and when I got there, I wasn't alone. The paramedics were there, and so was a Dr. Burt Winston. I didn't know him, but he was a member of the club. As I discovered later, the fellows I was playing cards with had called the 911 emergency number. They suspected something was wrong. Unfortunately, they were correct.

A stroke. I had had a stroke. Mel told my wife, Dutchie, when he got to the house that he was afraid I'd had a stroke, and he was exactly right. To this day, I haven't felt any pain. To this day, I don't really know what a stroke is. I do know that I went to Desert Hospital from my home in an ambulance and that I never lost consciousness. Dutchie's theory is that those exercises I did every morning might have pulled me through. I was too heavy, 236 pounds, but in relatively good shape otherwise. Thank God. Thank God for a lot of things.

When I awakened the next morning in the hospital, Dutchie was there. So were my sons, Skip and Chris, who had flown in—Skip from Atlanta, Chris from St. Louis. Also there was Sylvia Stein, the wife of my good friend Ben from Chicago. She just happened to be staying with us at the house when I took ill.

Dr. Winston confirmed that I'd had a stroke, whatever that was. I realized, lying there in bed, that I couldn't move my right arm or my right leg. I could talk, though. I thought I was coherent, but I wasn't. I was talking, but apparently nobody could understand me. It was an eerie feeling. I always figured I'd drop dead at the ballpark someday, yelling, "Cubs Win! Cubs Win!" with my last breath. I certainly didn't know what to make of this stroke business.

But I can honestly say that my first thought was, When can I get back to work? It was almost time for me to head to the Cubs' spring-training headquarters in Mesa, Arizona. We'd be doing our first broadcast of the Cactus League exhibition games in a couple weeks, and that's all that was on my mind. I don't remember being scared and I don't remember thinking to myself, Am I going to die? Of course, I did have my moments of depression, especially during the first week in the hospital, but that's where the fans came to my rescue.

You know, in all my years of broadcasting major-league baseball—twenty-five seasons with the St. Louis Cardinals, one with the Oakland Athletics, eleven with the Chicago White Sox, and since 1982 with the Cubs—there's only been one real criticism of my style. I like to mention names of viewers and listeners or even fans in attendance during the ball game.

"Happy Birthday to So-and-So." "Happy Anniversary to So-and-So." That's always been my way of acknowledging the fans, whether they're actually there at the stadium that day or tuning in. It doesn't take that much effort, and it certainly is harmless. Besides, you never know when you just might say something to someone to lift a person's spirits.

When someone sends a note up to the booth and then I read it on the air, it can make that person a big man or big woman on campus that day. He or she goes back home and friends will say, "Hey, Harry Caray was talking about you during the ball game this afternoon." In all my years, I never missed a pitch or a batter or an inning, so what's wrong with saying something about Joe Blow? Particularly if Joe Blow happens to be a shut-in who might be feeling down and just lives for those broadcasts.

Well, lying there in Desert Hospital, I realized that the shoe was on the other foot. There I was, stuttering and stammering, and here came the mail. Boxes and boxes of letters and telegrams and cards. Flowers, everything. From people I knew, but mostly from complete strangers. I stopped counting at fifteen thousand. There was no way to answer those people personally, except to get back to work. I realized then that I'd been right all along, despite what the critics said. If I ever lacked the motivation to make it back to the booth, those get-well wishes from everywhere really spurred me on. I was determined to broadcast baseball again.

After about a week, I started working with a speech therapist, Dr. Helene Kalfuss, but I needed only three sessions. When you have a stroke, your tongue becomes weak, and it becomes hard for you to enunciate. But I was doing okay. The therapist gave me lists of tongue twisters. Then she would have me speak extemporaneously. When I finally left the hospital, after about a month, I talked into a tape recorder at home. When there was a ball game on TV, I'd turn down the sound and do a couple of mock innings to myself. It sounded strange to me, kind of dead because there was no crowd. But one day I sort of just went off on my own. . . .

"Here we are in Philadelphia . . . Cubs leading three–two in the eighth inning . . . man on first base . . ." And so on.

"That's great," said Dutchie, who was listening. "You're back."

Well, at least I was headed back to the ballpark. I had my first look at the 1987 Cubs right there in Palm Springs during the third week in March when they came through to play the California Angels. I went out to both games, and it was great to see everybody again. I shook a lot of hands and said a lot of hellos. At that point, I was feeling so much better that Dr. Winston said I probably could broadcast again on Opening Day in Wrigley Field, April 7.

I thought about it, but by that time, WGN, which televises the Cubs in Chicago, had lined up guest announcers for the first few weeks of the season to work with Steve Stone, my outstanding partner on Channel 9. Brent Musburger of CBS was scheduled for the first game, followed by movie stars like Bill Murray, syndicated columnist George Will, and professional broadcasters such as Bob Costas from NBC, Ernie Harwell from Detroit, Jack Buck from St. Louis, and Pat Summerall of CBS. A different personality from a different walk of life every day.

I didn't want my streak of never having missed an inning in forty-four years to end, but WGN had made plans. Besides, there was my health to think about. I felt pretty good, but I figured if I took a little longer to get ready, then I'd be that much stronger when I did return. We decided that May 19 would be the day, the start of another Cubs' home stand. Meanwhile, Jim Dowdle, the head of WGN, was kind enough to have a satellite dish installed at our house in Palm Springs so I could keep track of the Cubs.

I appreciated that, and I got a real bang out of the parade of Steve's sidekicks. I was particularly proud of Steve. He was terrific. One day, he'd have a guy next to him who wanted to do some play-by-play. The next day, Steve would do the play-by-play while the guest did just the commentary or color. I watched it all, and when the Cubs were done with their day game at home, I'd tune in my son Skip, broadcasting the Atlanta Braves at night over their superstation, WTBS. I had plenty of baseball.

I'd been really itchy and anxious to get back to work for months, though, and I was more than ready when the time came to fly back to Chicago. I planned to try to sneak into town a week or so early. I had a lot of things to do—visit my dentist, my eye doctor, and so forth. It was arranged to have a private jet fly Dutchie and me back to Chicago, which took about six hours. Then Dutchie and I hopped in Ben Stein's limousine at O'Hare Airport and headed to the Ambassador East, where we live when we're in Chicago.

Everything was peaceful until we approached the intersection of Goethe and State Streets, where the hotel is. Then I saw a big banner welcoming me back, which was the idea of Dave Colella, the manager of the hotel. Then I saw a crowd of people, television cameras, and microphones. I was dead tired after that long trip. All I wanted to do was get into the room and go to sleep. But it was awfully nice to be back in Chicago, even if my return obviously wasn't a secret.

My Opening Day, May 19, was hard to remember and hard to forget, if that makes any sense. So many things happened that day. From the moment my good friend George Justak dropped me off outside Wrigley Field in the morning, I was surrounded by people, mostly fans just wanting to shake hands or get an autograph and wish me well. I went onto the field to record our pregame show for WGN Radio with Gene Michael, who was then manager of the Cubs. Then I went upstairs to prepare for the telecast of the Cubs versus the Cincinnati Reds. I was back to work again, and it felt great.

As we neared game time, I got a call in the booth from our production truck down below. It was Arne Harris, WGN-TV's brilliant director. He said Washington had called and might be calling back. Washington, as in Washington, D.C., and President Ronald Reagan.

"Arne," I said. "Iran just shot at a couple of our boats. I think the president has other things on his mind."

"Be ready," Arne said.

We went on the air, and I tried not to make a big thing of my return. I don't recall what I said to start the telecast—I'm the worst one to ask when it comes to recalling what I say. I probably said something about how it was a beautiful day at the ballpark, because that's what it was. Governor James Thompson of Illinois, who was there, had proclaimed it Harry Caray Day, which was nice. Everybody was nice to me. But the nicest part was just being there. The green grass was just as pretty as ever, and I was thrilled. I knew nothing had changed when Steve lit up one of those rotten-smelling cigars of his.

We weren't more than a few minutes into the game when Arne talked to me on the earphone.

"Harry," Arne said, "stand by. I have a phone call for you."

Sure enough, it was President Reagan calling from the White

House, right on the air. I had received a letter from him when I was hospitalized in Palm Springs, but for the president of the United States to take time to call me at Wrigley Field on a Tuesday afternoon was unbelievable. I was overwhelmed.

Ronald Reagan, of course, broadcast baseball for WHO in Iowa many years ago, before he became a successful actor in Hollywood. In fact, Mr. Reagan helped me broadcast a game in St. Louis. I want to say it was 1947. He came to town to plug his latest movie, *The Winning Team*, in which he played Grover Cleveland (Pete) Alexander, the pitcher who led the Cardinals to their first World Series title in 1926. Alexander won the second and sixth games of the Series, then saved the seventh game against the New York Yankees when Babe Ruth was thrown out trying to steal second base.

Anyway, here was this handsome young actor—Ronald Reagan—dropping by our broadcast booth in St. Louis forty years ago to say a few words. I remember asking him if he wanted to do play-by-play for a half-inning, and he said yes. I could tell he was good the moment I heard him. Then I prevailed upon him to do another half-inning, and another half-inning after that. He really enjoyed himself, but after two innings he looked at his watch. He had to go. Little did I imagine that *President* Ronald Reagan would call me in the booth at Wrigley Field some forty years later.

But that's the kind of day it was for me. It's been part of my routine in Chicago to sing "Take Me Out to the Ball Game" during the seventh-inning stretch at home games. I started doing it at Comiskey Park with the White Sox, and continued it at Wrigley Field with the Cubs. Well, on that May 19, in the top of the seventh inning, I could hear the fans warming up.

"HAR-RY! HAR-RY! HAR-RY!"

There was a big crowd for a Tuesday afternoon, about thirty

thousand or so, and by the time the middle of the seventh inning rolled around, I was overcome. Overwhelmed. I thought I was going to break up. I stood up in the booth, the whole ballpark seemed to turn to me, and I began singing into the public-address microphone. I don't think anybody heard me because the chanting and then the singing was so loud, which is just as well. You'd have to be a lot colder an individual than I am not to have been affected by the warmth those fans showed me. It was unbelievable. Not only that, the Cubs beat the Reds that day, 9–2.

As the weeks went on, I felt progressively more comfortable. Some people asked me why I went right back to a full work load—the first three and last three innings on TV, the middle three on radio—just the way I always had. Why didn't I ease back into things? Why did I go on the road with the Cubs right away instead of doing just home games?

Well, the reasons are simple. I wanted to and felt I could. I was bored when I wasn't doing what I wanted to do. I wanted to be working. Sure, it can be a grind, baseball day after day, but I'd been doing it practically all my life. I had gone from a guy who almost died to a guy doing baseball play-by-play in just over two months, and I was pretty damn happy about it. There weren't any days when I didn't feel like going to the ballpark. There never are.

The Tribune Company, which owns the Cubs and WGN, again was very good to me. It provided me a limousine on the road. I was picked up to go to the ballpark and then driven back to the hotel right after the game, along with whoever else from our crew wanted a ride. That was a big plus, because I was able to take off five minutes after we went off the air. Normally, I would have hopped the team bus, but that would have meant leaving the hotel two-and-a-half hours before the first pitch and leaving the ballpark an hour after the last pitch. Fortunately, the limo was also available to take us out to dinner, and so forth.

I thoroughly enjoyed getting back into the grind. The adrenaline was flowing again, and everywhere I went, I ran into friends I'd made throughout the years. I was happy to see them, and they were happy to see me looking so good after the stroke. I was down to about 188 pounds, drinking less and enjoying it just as much as when I'd been drinking a lot. The doctor never said I couldn't have a drink; he just cautioned me to exercise moderation. I discovered that wasn't so hard to do.

In the past, the only time I ever said no when somebody offered me a drink was when I didn't hear the question. I'd have a few Budweisers at the ballpark during the day, then maybe I'd have four or six drinks after the game, then I'd go home and have a few more, and then I'd go out for a late dinner and have a few more. I never got high, it never impaired my judgment, and believe me, in my heavy-drinking days, I took on some big-time thirsts and was able to drink them all under the table. And without getting drunk myself. I never got drunk, I just got happier.

My new routine was a lot more reserved. I'd have maybe a beer before dinner, maybe a gin martini or two with dinner and an after-dinner drink. That was it, and I found out I was having just as much fun. Another habit you get into in baseball is eating late at night. I never could eat before I went to work, so if we had a night game on the road, that meant having a big meal with drinks at one or two in the morning, then going to bed at three or four with all that food and booze just sitting there. It wasn't only bad for my digestion, it added a lot of pounds. Both are bad for your health.

I discovered, though, the less you drink, the less you want to eat. I'm no doctor, but I imagine your stomach shrinks and your appetite subsides when you drink less alcohol. Something like that. It only stands to reason. When I got back into the mainstream in 1987, I made sure to eat earlier than usual—whether I broadcast a day game at home or a night game on the road—and eat lighter. Some chicken or a little pasta, a salad, and nothing more. I used to be a big steak eater, but I cut down on my meat. I also used to be an ice-cream freak, so I had to start watching that and all dairy products. Breakfast was no problem. I was never a big breakfast guy. One poached egg in the morning is enough.

After a few months of moderation, I was used to it. I thought the same way, broadcast the same way, and my personality hadn't changed, I don't think. I might have been a little more boring, standing around nursing one drink, but otherwise, I had no problems with my new diet. My blood pressure was good and my weight steady. Hell, if I'd have done this all my life, I'd have probably been the president of IBM.

Dutchie mentioned to me that I'd probably been using drinking as a crutch all those years, and she might have had a point. I was probably more nervous than I cared to admit, or at least more wound up, more hyperactive. I was always dead tired after broadcasting a game, and the reason was, I always put so much into it. Every game to me was the seventh game of the World Series. I admire those broadcasters now who can do an entire game, and when they come out of the booth, they aren't sweating, there isn't a hair out of place, and their neckties are still perfectly knotted. Me, it looks as though I've played in the game, or gone fifteen rounds.

That doesn't mean I've been doing it right and they've been doing it wrong. It's just a matter of styles, and invariably, as tired as I was after a game, I'd use alcohol to wind down. Plus, I had taken a lot of aspirin for an arthritic back. On those TV commercials, they tell you that aspirin is great for preventing heart attacks, but they don't tell you that aspirin can tear a hole in your stomach. I wound up with a bleeding ulcer after the 1984 season. That was the year the Cubs won the National League East title, then the first two games of the best-of-five play-off against the San Diego Padres, only to lose three straight games in San Diego and the pennant.

I didn't feel all that sick after the play-off was over, but I guess I was. I thought it was just the fast pace, the trauma of losing, the excitement of wanting to win, and the fact that I was eating more, drinking more, and sleeping less. But when I got back to Chicago from San Diego, I went in for a checkup and right into the hospital.

Then came the stroke of 1987. You know, at Wrigley Field there's a ramp that you have to climb to get from field level to the broadcast booth. No elevators or escalators at Wrigley Field. When I returned from Palm Springs in May, Dr. Jacob Suker, the Cubs' team physician, was concerned about whether I could make that climb. There was a plan to transport me back and forth from upstairs to downstairs on a golf cart. But I did a dry run before the day I returned to the broadcast booth for real, and I realized it was easier for me than before I got sick. I was actually in better health. In the past, I would walk upstairs and wind up huffing and puffing. I'd stop along the way, as if because I had autographs to sign, but the main reason was to catch my breath.

After I lost all that weight, that ramp was a lot easier for me to handle. And no wonder. Try taking a walk like that with a forty-pound weight strapped on your back, and then try without it. Which is easier? That's how I felt with my new body, my Robert Redford body. I was feeling a lot better, and still having my fun.

The only thing wrong about my return to the WGN television and radio booth in 1987 was the way the Cubs played. They were very disappointing. Pitcher Rick Sutcliffe won 18 games and almost won the Cy Young Award in the National League, and Andre Dawson, whom the Cubs signed as a free agent from the Montreal Expos in spring training, hit 49 home runs and batted in 137 runs to win the Most Valuable Player Award. Yet the Cubs still finished in last place, and didn't look real good doing it!

But it was great to be back, nevertheless. I don't know what I would have done if I hadn't been able to broadcast baseball again. I never really gave it much thought. I would probably have liked to do something involving people. Or I might have done some traveling. I haven't been around the world. I've been to Europe only once, when I visited France, England, and Germany. But, I've never been to Italy and a lot of other places. Certainly, Dutchie deserves a trip like that.

I don't know what to say about Dutchie except that if I loved her before my illness, I love her ten times more afterward. She is a wonderful woman. She was very supportive during my recuperation, yet she didn't baby me for a moment. Too few times in life, people are able to show what they're really made of. She certainly showed me during those couple months. She was beside me every day when she really could have said, "I've had enough of this." I got depressed and down a few times, but Dutchie and all that mail I got and my doctors—Dr. Winston in Palm Springs and Dr. Gerry Smythe in Chicago—pulled me through.

After the season, during the winter, I was asked to go to Denver to attend the convention of the National Stroke Association. I was honored as their Man of the Year for what I had done. From a hospital bed to the broadcast booth in just a couple of months. I met a lot of other stroke victims there, people in wheelchairs, people who were really feeling down and out, people who had been through what I'd been through but who hadn't been as fortunate.

I'm not so sure, though, that I deserved any trophies for what I had done. I am not a religious man. I've made some mistakes in life. Dutchie is my third wife, I have children by my first two marriages, and I've paid a lot of alimony in my time. But I've always believed in the Almighty God. I've always believed that if you live your life as a decent person, the umpire in the end will say you did it right.

I've tried to be kind and compassionate and decent and caring. And the Lord must think I've been a pretty good human being, because he's been so good to me. He was awfully good to me in 1987. I know that, and I'll never forget it.

RUNS HITS CHAPTER

0 0 2

 It was grade-school graduation day for me in St. Louis. All the boys in the Dewey School graduating class were wearing blue coats and white flannel pants. All the boys except me, that is. I didn't own a pair of white pants, and I sure couldn't afford to go out and buy them. So I wore what I already had, what I wore every day—plain gray pants.

The other kids really gave it to me. They badgered and ridiculed—and believe me, nothing is crueler than the humor of young children. They couldn't possibly have known the hurt, the embarrassment, I felt. I'm sure they thought I was deliberately being different, while I, of course, would never admit that I was simply too poor to conform.

So on that day it was Laugh, clown, laugh, even though your heart is breaking, laugh. I don't remember if I really *was* able to laugh. I doubt it, because my heart really was breaking. But through the pain, through the tears, I made a solemn vow.

Never again would I be unable to afford a pair of white pants. Or blue ones or red ones or plaid ones, if that's what I felt like wearing. I decided then and there that eventually I'd be able to buy as many pairs of white pants as I wanted. I honestly believe that my desire for personal success began on that never-to-be-forgotten day of humiliation.

Which leads to one of the common themes that's seemed to run throughout my life and, as you'll see, throughout this book: Just when I think I've hit bottom, when something has happened that I'm sure is the worst thing that can possibly occur, it always leads to something good. Everything good that has happened to me has happened as a direct result of something bad.

For instance, I used to be the announcer for the St. Louis Cardinals baseball club. But after I'd been twenty-five years on the job, my contract was not renewed. I was let go. Maybe you heard about it.

Well, at the time, I thought that was absolutely the worst thing that could ever happen to me. I mean, for twenty-five seasons I was the voice of that team, a team with every bit as much pride and tradition as any in the game, including the Yankees, Dodgers, Cubs, or Red Sox. I was sure that would be the only broadcasting job I'd ever have, doing baseball games for the St. Louis Cardinals.

Boy, was I wrong about that. I felt terrible when it happened, and I was wrong about that, too. As I said, it turned out to be a bad experience that produced a lot of good.

Like what?

Well, shortly after the announcement, I was contacted by Charles O. Finley, then the owner of the Oakland A's. I met with him in his office in Chicago, and I learned my first important lesson since the Cardinals had cut me loose—I had been a bad businessman for a lot of years.

To induce me to come to Oakland, Finley offered me thirty thousand dollars more than I'd been making while working for the Cardinals. He also offered me a penthouse apartment and a Cadillac. By the time I returned to St. Louis a few days later, the pain was still there, but it was eased by the fact that I was now quite a bit richer.

When I got out to Oakland, something else happened that was important in my life. I found I could be as good a broadcaster for the A's as I had been for the Cardinals. That might sound a little silly to you, but don't forget, I had been born and raised in St. Louis. I'd been a Cardinal fan for as long as I could remember. I was sure that had something to do—a *lot* to do—with the excitement and enthusiasm I brought to my Cardinal broadcasts.

Plus, in the National League, I had been brainwashed about the inferiority of the American League. I really wasn't convinced that I could overcome all this. I didn't know if I could be the same dynamic announcer for a team I knew nothing about and cared little for, in a league that I believed wasn't as good as the one I'd left.

Well, I hadn't been broadcasting in Oakland for a month when I realized it's the *game* that I love. It's *baseball*. It's the *players*. It's not a particular team or league. It wasn't a month before I came to care about the young ballplayers Finley had assembled the same way I cared about the Cardinal players I'd spent a quarter of a century with.

Finley had formed a fine young nucleus of players, a nucleus that would evolve into a dynasty during the 1970's—Sal Bando, Catfish Hunter, Reggie Jackson, Bert Campaneris, Don

Mincher, Joe Rudi, Dick Green, Blue Moon Odom, Rollie Fingers, among others. It was a new team of new players in a new league, and I was just as excited as I'd ever been.

The good comes from the bad. Works every time.

So do luck and desire, two other ingredients to life that I think dominate everything else.

I've been extremely lucky in a lot of ways. But I'm also pretty sure that my strong desire forced a lot of that good fortune. It's kind of like the chicken and the egg. It's hard to determine which came first. It's also hard to know which is more important. But I do know you need both. And if you *have* both, you can do just about anything.

I don't like to preach, but one of the great things about America is that this is truly the land of opportunity. If you've got those magic intangibles, luck and desire, then throw in a little guts, some timing, confidence, common sense, and faith, you're going to succeed.

That doesn't mean there won't be roadblocks. It doesn't mean things will come easily, without a struggle. But they'll come.

I know. I've been down—way down—and up. Then I've been down again and up again.

Which once again brings me back to my leaving the Cardinals. I may as well tell the story now. It's an important part of my life, and it's what people want to know about.

A little background:

Long before the Dallas Cowboys played a game, long before a fellow named Ted Turner would make my oldest son, Skip, his broadcaster, and put the Atlanta Braves on his superstation, back in the days when there were sixteen major-league baseball clubs and none west of St. Louis, my team—the Cardinals—was America's Team.

For a quarter of a century, on more than two hundred radio stations from Florida all the way to California, you could listen to me describe the exploits of so many of the game's great players like Stan Musial and Terry Moore and Red Schoendienst and Marty Marion and Enos Slaughter and Harry Brecheen and Howie Pollet.

I was born and raised in St. Louis, and for as long as I could remember, baseball had been the most important thing in my life. It filled a lot of emptiness for me. It filled a great void in my life. And I loved it. There were times when I probably loved it a little too much, loved it more than I loved anything else. I paid the price for that—a couple of busted marriages, too much time away from my kids when they were growing up—but still, my affection for the game, and especially for the Cardinals, never wavered.

When I was still a kid, twenty-five, no older than any of the players, I became a baseball announcer in St. Louis. Within a couple of years, I was the Cardinals' only play-by-play man, their voice. Through three owners—Sam Breaden, Fred Saigh, and Gussie Busch—through eleven managers and almost as many broadcast partners, I never missed a game.

So, you can imagine, by 1969 I should have felt pretty secure with the St. Louis baseball Cardinals.

We were family. The team had played in the World Series three times in the last six seasons. Our attendance was terrific. The club had drawn over a million fans for seven years in a row. In two of the pennant-winning years, 1967 and 1968, the Cardinals drew over 2 million. I was a heck of a salesman for the club, and I was a darn good beer salesman to boot, which is no small thing when you're working for a ball club that is owned by the world's biggest brewery, Anheuser-Busch.

I really felt that I was an integral part of the Cardinals' recent successes. I was proud of what we had accomplished together. It had been a real good twenty-five years. And I was looking forward to another twenty-five.

Then, just when I thought they were going to give me a gold watch for twenty-five years' work, they gave me a pink slip.

To tell the truth, I was not completely surprised when the Cardinals decided not to renew my contract.

For several months, I'd been hearing stories at home and on the road. There were all kinds of rumors going around about me. The most spectacular rumors were all about sex. I was allegedly having an affair with this executive's wife or that executive's wife.

At first, these rumors annoyed me. Then they began to amuse me. They actually made me feel kind of good. I mean, let's face it. I was almost fifty years old. I wore glasses as thick as the bottoms of Bud bottles, and as much as I hate to say it, I was never confused with Robert Redford. Yet it seemed like half of St. Louis and nearly the entire National League thought that no young, beautiful woman could resist my charms.

If you were me, would *you* have gone around denying rumors like that?

Hell, no.

So I didn't deny them.

If anyone asked me point-blank, I had a stock line. "I never raped anybody in my life," I'd say.

It was certainly true, and it usually got a laugh. But I got a little worried that the Cardinals weren't laughing, so I went to see Gussie Busch.

We had been friends since he had bought the ball club back in 1953. I liked Gussie and respected him, and I felt I should try to clear the air.

I went to his office at the brewery and told him I was concerned about these rumors.

Gussie started to laugh.

"I've heard your response to these rumors. You've never raped anybody, right, Harry?"

"That's right," I replied and started to laugh, too.

"Well, if it's not rape, then it's mutual consent. And if that's the case, you've got nothing to worry about."

But I did worry.

On the road, other broadcasters would tell me they'd been asked to submit audition tapes to the Cardinals because there was supposed to be an opening coming up.

And one day, the *Post-Dispatch*, the big afternoon newspaper in St. Louis, owned by the Pulitzer family, ran a story confirming that I would not be returning to the Cards after the season ended.

Still no one had said a word to me—not the station, not the brewery, not even the advertising agency.

But I've always been a realist, and I know that where there's smoke, there's usually fire. So, on the last day of the season, the first place I stopped when I got to the ballpark was the Stadium Club. I had a special request for Marty Marion, the great Cardinal shortstop of the 1940's, who was the Stadium Club manager at the time.

"Who knows?" I said to Marty. "This might be my last day here. And if it is, I want the fellows on the team to have a little something to remember me by. As soon as the game is over, send a couple of cases of champagne down to the clubhouse and charge 'em to my account."

It was still hours before the game, so I then headed straight for the clubhouse. I wanted to shake hands with everyone and wish them all well for the winter. That's something I have pretty much always done. Before the first game of the season, I wish everyone good luck, and after the last game I bid them all good-bye. Between those days, I try to stay *out* of the clubhouse.

Anyway, that day when I was down shaking hands and bidding my adieux, I ran into Jack Buck. Now Jack and I had been partners since 1954, the first year Anheuser-Busch sponsored Cardinals' broadcasts. He's an outstanding broadcaster—one of the best who ever lived—and to this day he's a good friend. But friend or not, I had a feeling he might have known something.

Once we'd stepped out of the clubhouse, into a corridor, where we could have a little privacy, I turned to Jack.

"Jack," I began, "we've been through some trying personal experiences together. I've proved my friendship to you, and I'll always consider you one of my friends. But I have to ask you, do you know something that I should know?"

He mumbled that he really didn't know anything.

"I know about the audition tapes," I said, and hearing this, Jack broke down and spilled the beans. He revealed that Al Fleishman and Bob Hyland had asked him to recruit other announcers. He didn't like it, but he'd had to do it.

Well, Fleishman—whose public-relations agency still represents Anheuser-Busch—and I had been enemies for decades, going back to the days when he was the St. Louis Browns' publicity man. He'd once said that if he could get rid of Harry Caray, the Browns could run the Cardinals out of town. It was a little late to do the defunct Browns any good, but it looked as if he was finally getting his wish.

Hyland, on the other hand, was an old and dear friend, instrumental in my career and in my son Skip's, and one of the truly great radio executives ever. He was—still is, in fact—the general manager of KMOX, which, through the years, has probably been the best-run radio station in the country.

"Harry, I should have talked to you," Buck admitted sadly. "But confrontation is not my style, and I've been asked to keep it secret."

If the situation had been reversed, I would have told Jack all I knew, but I understood where Jack was coming from. And as soon as he told me about Fleishman and Hyland, I knew it was all over, that it was just a matter of time.

Actually, it was a matter of about three weeks.

It happened about one o'clock on a late October afternoon, after the play-offs and the World Series were over. I was sitting in the Cinema Bar, a nice saloon above a theater across from the ballpark and about a block from KMOX, where I still went to work every afternoon to do the drive-time sports report at five-thirty. I was sitting with an old friend of mine, Tom Sullivan, who was visiting St. Louis from California. We were having a few beers and reminiscing about old times when the telephone rang.

Frank Ceresia, the owner of the Cinema as well as a bartender there, hollered that it was for me. I was surprised. Who knows I'm here? I thought to myself.

It was Don Hamel, another old friend.

"Don," I said, "how the hell did you find me here?"

Hamel, who had been on the job for only a short while, was the advertising manager for Busch Bavarian beer, the sponsor of the Cardinals' broadcasts. Before that, he had been general manager of a radio station in town. He astutely pointed out that we had spent a lot of nights in a lot of the same places.

"I know your drinking habits pretty well." He laughed.

I had to agree.

Then he got down to business.

"Harry," he almost whispered, "I don't know how to put this to you. We're good friends, and I've only been in this job a month, and why the hell they picked me to tell you this I don't know. But they're going to make an announcement at two o'clock in which they state that they're not going to renew your contract."

So, after twenty-five years of never missing a game, of being the most loyal Cardinal supporter on the face of the earth, I got fired over the telephone in a saloon. It was probably appropriate, but I couldn't really appreciate the irony at the time.

Hamel read the press release to me. In it, they explained that the determination not to renew my contract as the Cardinals' broadcaster was "the decision of the marketing department" of Anheuser-Busch.

"Don," I had to ask, after he finished reading the release, "who's the best beer salesman you've ever met?"

"Harry," he replied—and honestly, too, I've got to give him that—"you ask that question of anybody in the business, and they'll say you are."

The crazy thing was, if there was one thing in the world that proved my prowess as a beer peddler, it was Busch Bavarian beer, which is now simply called Busch.

Busch was introduced out of nowhere in 1955. When the brewery made its big push, they sent me over to the Bavarian Alps to film television commercials. After a time, they made it the principal sponsor of the Cardinals' games, replacing Budweiser. And the strategy worked. Busch became the first new beer in many, many years to be introduced successfully by an American brewery. Today, it is still probably the biggest-selling beer in St. Louis, bigger even than Bud. Yet here was Anheuser-Busch, saying that the marketing department had decided I wasn't doing the proper job for the product.

"They wanted you to know this before you heard it on the air," Hamel said. "I did, too."

In somewhat of a daze, I thanked him, hung up, and asked Frank to turn the radio to KMOX.

KMOX was then, and still is, all-talk radio. They made the announcement just as Hamel said they would, on the two o'clock newscast, then they went back to their regularly scheduled programming. Unfortunately for them, the program happened to be an open-line call-in show. Listeners could call up and talk about whatever was on their minds.

Much to my delight, it was "bombs away!"

The calls started pouring in, and they were all about Harry Caray. This was not the way the station or the brewery had planned it.

As I understand it, Bob Hyland, the general manager, had instructed the girl screening the calls to refuse anyone who wanted to talk about Harry Caray. Only this wasn't as simple as it seemed, because *every* call was about Harry Caray. Every single one. When they put fourteen calls on hold and every button on the telephone console was flashing, then they had no choice but to put that next call on the air. The fifteenth call was about Harry Caray, too.

After a while, Hyland apparently was beside himself. He called down to this poor girl and yelled, "Dammit, didn't I tell you not to take any more calls about Harry Caray?"

And she yelled back, "Mr. Hyland, *all* the calls are about Harry Caray. If you think you can do better, you come down and handle this yourself. Because I quit!" And she hung up the receiver.

It hadn't taken more than a few minutes for my departure to become a cause célèbre in St. Louis. It was the biggest story in town.

On my way back home that night, I stopped, as I often did, at a restaurant and bar called Busch's Grove—which, despite its name, has no association with the brewery. It's a nice place where all the locals hung out, right near my home in St. Louis's western suburbs.

When I got there, the television stations started calling. They wanted to interview me for the evening news. I told them that I'd just left downtown. If they wanted to see me, they'd have to come out to Busch's Grove. That's where the Harry Caray Firing Headquarters had been set up.

That's when I did the only thing I wish I hadn't. My anger began to grow, and with the television stations coming out, I decided to get some revenge at the brewery.

I knew they didn't carry Schlitz at Busch's Grove and, frankly, it would have been about the last beer I would have thought to order. But at the time, Schlitz was Anheuser-Busch's big competition. So I asked Otis Dunlap, the bartender, to go across the street and buy a six-pack of Schlitz for me.

Some of my friends, notably Tom Sullivan, tried to talk me out of it. They insisted that I really shouldn't go through with my plan. They pointed out that I owned a lot of Anheuser-Busch stock (which I do to this day), and that the brewery had made me a wealthy man. But I was stubborn. I wouldn't listen.

"When those television stations come here," I said, "I want to have a can of Schlitz in my hand, and a six-pack right on my table!"

So Otis got the Schlitz. And when the television crews and the photographers showed up, there I was. It was a strange and famous picture: Harry Caray holding a can of Schlitz. But I didn't drink from it.

I thought it was funny at the time. Because I was angry and hurt, it seemed like the right gesture to make. But now I realize it was petty. Because, to tell the truth, I never drank Schlitz before that day or that day, and I've never had a Schlitz since.

But that is the only regret I have about what happened that day. The good comes from the bad, remember? Although I surely didn't realize it then, getting my release from the St. Louis Cardinals didn't hurt me at all. It opened the door to other opportunities.

Because my contract wasn't renewed, I got to spend a summer in Oakland, working for Charles Finley and watching the birth of those great A's teams.

Then I moved to Chicago, my kind of town. First came the years with the White Sox, with Bill Veeck and Chuck Tanner and Richie Allen. Wonderful years.

And now I'm with the Cubs. I get to go to work every day in a magical place called Wrigley Field, where they play baseball the way God intended for it to be played, on real grass, and except for a few night games now, in the real sunshine.

Luck and desire.

I've had both of them on my side. There isn't really too much for me to complain about.

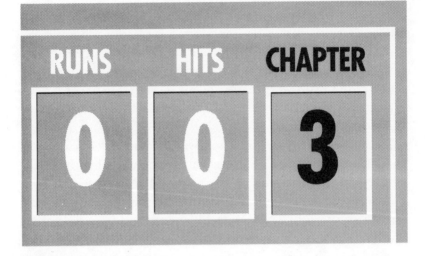

RUNS   HITS   CHAPTER

0   0   3

I have never talked much about my childhood. I'm not going to spend a lot of time on it here, because there isn't much to talk about. The human mind has a mechanism that forces you—or enables you, as the case may be—to forget unpleasant experiences. With me, that mechanism has wiped out great parts of my early years. I simply do not remember a lot of names or dates or places. In some sense, it's fortunate—I was not particularly happy then— and in some ways, it's unfortunate. Who knows exactly what's been lost?

I was born Harry Christopher Carabina in St. Louis, Missouri. My father was Christopher Carabina. He was Italian; that's about all I know for sure. I don't know what he did, except disappear. I don't know where he lived. I don't know when he died. I never met the man.

My mother was the former Daisy Argint. She was Rumanian. When I was five or six years old, she remarried. A year or two later, when I was seven or eight, she died. I didn't know my stepfather very well. He ran a restaurant, I think. He tried to keep me after my mother died, but that didn't work out.

So I was sent to live with my mother's brother. He was married to a woman named Doxie—which would make her my aunt—and they had four children of their own. Not long after I got there, my uncle disappeared. I don't even know what happened to him. He either deserted his family or died. All I know is that I was raised by my aunt, Doxie.

We lived at 1909 LaSalle Street. Why I remember that address, I don't know. But I do. I remember it as a tough neighborhood, but the people who lived there—mostly Italians, Irish, and Syrians—were proud and hard-working and they kept the neighborhood meticulously clean. Still, compared to our neighborhood, the Hill (the tough Italian area nearby where Yogi Berra and Joe Garagiola grew up) was Beverly Hills.

But to this day, I still go back to 1909 LaSalle Street every once in a while when I'm in St. Louis, particularly if Dutchie is with me on the trip. I drive around to see what is left of my past. I suppose I also go there to remind myself of the road I've traveled, of the opportunities I've taken advantage of. I remind myself that I started with nothing and made it as high as I've wanted to go.

The neighborhood, which got a little shabby at one point, looks surprisingly good. They've rebuilt it, and I get a kick out of going back there. Dutchie and I have even talked about buying 1909 LaSalle Street if it became available, just so I could say I bought the house I was raised in.

I don't know how the people in my old neighborhood look at things, whether they figure that life is playing a bad trick on them or what. But I do know that if they are willing to work hard and pursue a dream, if they are disciplined and fearless enough to take control of their own destiny, they can succeed and achieve that better life.

I know that because it is exactly what I did. It's why I'm such a believer in the land of opportunity. I've not only seen it, I've lived it.

What I remember most vividly of those early days is that I made my own way. I remember that, and I remember books. And I remember sports.

My first job was selling newspapers in the afternoon. This is when I was eight, nine, ten years old. I started at the corner of Eighteenth and Chouteau, a wiry little kid selling the evening *Post-Dispatch* to the workers who were getting off the day shift at the International Shoe Factory. Every day I would be there, hawking those newspapers. It didn't matter what the weather was. I didn't care whether it was freezing cold and snowing in the winter or hot and dripping with humidity in the summer. I was always shouting those headlines, enticing those workers with stories about cops and robbers, about politicians and businessmen, about movie stars and ballplayers. Looking back on it now, I have to wonder if that isn't where I got my start in broadcasting.

After a big day of hawking papers on the corner of Eighteenth and Chouteau, I would have maybe forty cents in my pocket. Rolling in dough! But I was careful about the money, so I established a little ritual.

When I sold out my papers, I'd head immediately for the lending library on the corner. Every night I would take out a book—it only cost three cents. Then I would stop at the soda fountain and have a chocolate-marshmallow sundae. That cost a dime. While I was eating that sundae, I could read a quarter or a third of the book. That night, when I went home, I would finish the book. I could also give any remaining money—usually twenty-five or thirty cents—to the family. The next day, I'd return the book, sell my newspapers, borrow another book, and stop for another chocolate-marshmallow sundae.

Reading those books—my favorites were the stories about Frank Merriwell, the fictitious Yale sports star—was probably how I developed my vocabulary, my interest in words, and perhaps even my desire and ability to communicate.

There is another part of my childhood that has stayed with me all my life: Christmas always has been a pensive and reflective time for me, and it probably always will be.

Even now, when I'm happily and thoroughly in love with Dutchie, I've got to get away at Christmas. On Christmas Day, I have to be alone with my thoughts. I have to be alone, period. I don't want to be with her family or with my children or grandchildren. For me, it's a melancholy time. I get away to Palm Springs to be by myself and escape with my thoughts, my feelings, my memories, and my fantasies of what could have been but never was.

Now I've never talked to a shrink about this. I've never been to one in my life. I just don't believe in them, though they might have the technical medical analysis of what it is I feel around Christmas. I would guess that it has something to do with depression, though. All I can tell you is that from the time I was a little kid, Christmas was a sad season for me because I didn't have what everybody else had. I never had a mother and father around. No brothers and sisters. I never had the toys and gifts under the tree that other children did.

I can afford to buy anything I want at Christmas now. But there is nothing that makes me feel any different. I guess the lesson this teaches is the old one, the simple one, the cliché, the one that people have to keep learning over and over again the hard way. Money can't necessarily buy happiness.

The first thing I fell deeply, passionately, madly, and irrevocably in love with as a young boy was the game of baseball. I loved to play it and to watch it, I loved to read about it, and perhaps most of all, I loved to talk about it, argue about it, analyze it.

Enter the St. Louis Cardinals into the life of Harry Caray.

From April until October, I was preoccupied with the Cardinals. As a schoolboy, I couldn't wait to get out of the classroom to find out whether they had won or lost. When I was a young man working at my first jobs, I usually rushed out of the office to find out how they had fared. My wildest fantasy was that someday I'd get to wear the Cardinals' uniform.

Whenever I had enough money, I'd go see the Cardinals play at old Sportsman's Park, out on Grand Avenue. I'd take a streetcar from LaSalle; the token was a nickel. Then—if I had enough money—I'd buy a hot dog outside the ballpark. They cost a dime, I think. And they were always so much better than the hot dogs sold inside the ballpark. They tasted better and they smelled better. They still do, at any ballpark, to this day.

I always sat in the bleachers then. I think a ticket was maybe half a buck.

I was a member of what was called the Knothole Gang. When the game was over, we would wait around the players' gate for autographs or, even better, we would go down on the field and run around. Things were different in those days. The ball clubs didn't have to worry about vandalism. To us, the field at Sportsman's Park was sacred turf. We worshiped the ground our idols, the ballplayers, worked on, and we would never have done anything destructive to it.

The biggest thrill was to take your place at home plate, pantomime a swing, sprint around first, and slide into second, safe with a double, just like Rogers Hornsby. Or maybe you took your position at shortstop, hustled to your right, made a backhanded stab, and—holy cow!—threw out the runner at first.

As I got older, I didn't have to pantomime for thrills. I became a pretty good little ballplayer. Not great. But pretty good.

By now I had moved out to Webster Groves, a suburb southwest of the city, to live with my aunt Doxie.

I was doing nicely as a student—a B-plus average—especially when you consider I couldn't afford to buy the necessary schoolbooks. My best subject was Spanish. I always got A's. Unfortunately, now I don't remember much of what I learned. I wish I did—with the emergence of so many great Latin-American ballplayers, it would be a tremendous help in my job.

While I have forgotten most of what they attempted to teach me in the classrooms of various schools, I do clearly remember the important lessons taught by a fellow named Froebel Gaines.

Froebel Gaines was the baseball coach at Webster High and an astute baseball mind. He knew the game very well. He knew how to deal with different personalities, too—something you really need to know these days to work in the major leagues. Froebel's not with us anymore, but he was a dear friend for a long time.

I played some second base and shortstop when I learned the game from Coach Gaines. He taught me the fundamentals as well as the intricacies. He also made a switch-hitter out of me. Eventually, I became a good enough ballplayer that I was offered a tuition scholarship by the University of Alabama. I couldn't accept it, though. I couldn't swing the room and board or the books and travel expense. I had to go to work to support myself when I graduated from high school.

For a while, supporting myself meant working at odd jobs. I tended bar, waited tables, sold newspapers. I was a gofer, a flunky at fight camps. Anything to make a few bucks to pay my way.

On the weekends, I played semipro ball, which was a good way to make a few more dollars. I was a second baseman and shortstop for teams with names like the Smith Undertakers and the Webster Groves Birds, and got fifteen or twenty dollars a game. I actually attracted the attention of some scouts. Once I was invited to one of the Cardinals' minor-league tryout camps over in Decatur, Illinois. They took a good look at me, had me there a couple of days. But I just didn't have the physical skills —the arm, the speed, the eyesight—to play ball professionally. Myopic little guys who build their reputation on hustle and savvy generally don't make it to the big leagues.

One of my teammates on the Webster Groves Birds was a fellow named Ray Higgins. He knew I was looking for regular work and offered me a job as his assistant. He had a very impressive job—sales manager of the Medart Manufacturing Company, which made products like basketball backboards and gymnastic equipment and school lockers. My job as the assistant to the sales manager was to dictate letters to agents and customers, solicit sales, and answer complaints. It was steady work and the pay was great, about twenty-five dollars a week!

And let me tell you, I needed every penny. I was married by now to my first wife, Dorothy, who had literally been the girl next door. All I had to do when I got married was move a few feet, from my aunt Doxie's house over to Dorothy's parents' place. Living with them was a considerable help to me financially.

Dorothy is a terrific woman, and she was a great wife. A wonderful mother to Skip and our two other children, Patricia and Christopher.

I, on the other hand, wasn't the world's greatest husband. Especially once I began broadcasting. I was hardly ever home, always on the road with this ball club or that one, hustling jobs here and there, making the scene, building my career as an announcer.

In 1949, Dorothy and I were divorced. To this day, I write her a monthly alimony check. And I can't say I really mind. She deserves it for putting up with me as long as she did. The divorce was completely my fault.

But in August 1979, I do remember noting our anniversary on one particular check. "Holy cow!" I wrote. "Thirty years. How much longer does this go on?"

And about a week later, I received a note written in elegant script on beautiful stationery.

> *Dearest Harry,*
>   *Till death do us part!*
>
>   *Love, Dorothy*

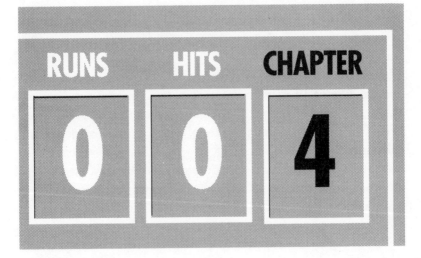

RUNS   HITS   CHAPTER

0   0   4

 I was putting in long hours at Medart during the week. I was still playing ball on the weekends. And I was trying to spend time with my new family. Yet I still found room in my life for my beloved Cardinals. Lots of room.

Whenever I could afford the money and the time, I went down to Sportsman's Park to watch them play. And when I couldn't do that, I listened to the broadcasts of their games on the big upright radio that was sitting in the living room.

Gradually, I noticed a difference in the games I heard and the games I saw. Whenever I went to the ballpark, it was a special occasion. From the minute batting practice started right up to the last pitch, being at the ballpark was an exciting experience for me.

Part of it, I'm sure, was that I was living vicariously through the players. They were doing what I had always dreamed of doing. They were getting the hits and making the plays that I only imagined I could.

But it was more than that. The ballpark had an ambiance that helped you forget your cares and woes. There was the uncertainty, the anticipation, even the *smell* of being around a ballpark. Back in those days, there was a distinctive fragrance that rose from a neighborhood ballpark. Freshly mowed grass . . . steaming hot dogs . . . beer and peanuts and popcorn. It was a wonderful aroma that came from the ballpark and seemed to envelop the entire neighborhood.

Somehow that fragrance is missing from the new ballparks nowadays, although we still have it in Chicago, on the South Side at Comiskey Park and especially on the North Side at Wrigley Field.

Anyway, every time I went to the ballpark—whether the Cardinals won or lost, whether the game was well played or not —I felt that excitement, I experienced that thrill. But when I stayed home and listened to the radio broadcasts, what I heard was as dull and boring as the morning crop reports.

I decided there had to be a better way.

So I wrote a letter to Merle Jones, the man who ran the biggest radio station in St. Louis—KMOX, a CBS-owned station—and pretty much told him why he should hire me to broadcast baseball. The Cardinals and St. Louis Browns were both in town then, and the Commissioner's Office allowed teams to broadcast only home games. Baseball then was operating under the incorrect assumption that broadcasting road games back to two-team cities would somehow hurt the attendance of the team playing at home that day. One of the visionaries who proved that theory wrong was Philip K. Wrigley, who not only had the games of his Cubs broadcast on several Chicago radio stations at the same time, he put Cub home games on local television. I believe that helped generations and generations of young people become Cub fans in their adult years. To this day, that's the case.

Now you have to understand a few things here. I didn't know anything about broadcasting. Nothing. I had never in my life seen a radio studio. Or even a microphone. But I was not about to let any of that stand in my way.

Desire and luck.

The desire was obvious: I wanted to be a baseball announcer. I loved the Cardinals, I loved the game. Heck, I can go across the street and watch a Little League game and enjoy it.

But here's the luck:

Instead of sending my letter to the radio station, I took the trouble of finding out Merle Jones's home address. It was 825 South Skinker. I remember that to this day and will remember it as long as I live. The address changed my whole life.

If I had sent the letter to Jones at his office, it more than likely would have gotten lost in the shuffle. But it arrived at 825 South Skinker Street on a Monday afternoon—the first Monday, Jones told me years later, that he ever had come home from the office early, that he ever had gotten to the mail before his wife, who was out when he arrived home.

Jones had had a long weekend entertaining some executives visiting from New York. He was dead tired, maybe a little hung over, so he'd left the office about two o'clock. He went straight home, fixed himself a scotch and soda, kicked off his shoes, and started flipping through the mail. He came to this letter marked PERSONAL, and rushed to open it. He didn't know whether it was good news or bad, but it looked important.

It was important, at least to me.

Apparently, Merle Jones got a terrific kick out of my letter.

He was impressed by my initiative. He was also relieved that the PERSONAL on the envelope was merely the way for an aggressive young job-seeker to get some attention, to get an audience.

So, the next day, Jones sent a response and invited me to his office for a meeting.

When I met with Merle Jones several days later, we had a nice, friendly chat. He listened to me explain to him exactly why I could do a much better job broadcasting a ball game than anybody. He said he'd give me the chance to prove it.

"The first thing we've got to do is find out about your voice," Jones explained. "So, I'm going to arrange an audition for you."

He called in his program director and told him, "I want you to give this young man an audition. And let me know when it's going to be, because I want personally to hear him."

Then Jones turned to me.

"I'll listen," he said. "Then I'll let you know whether I think you should give up your job and take a chance in this business or whether you should just pack up your dreams and keep working as a sales correspondent."

I thanked him profusely. Then I went home to study and worry for a week.

The program director had given me a script for what must have been the standard announcer's audition. It was a few news items, a few sports items, and a few about opera and classical music.

The news and the sports I could handle without much difficulty.

By the time the week had passed, however, I was sure I had worked long and hard enough to have it all down, to sound just the way a professional announcer for KMOX should sound.

I went in for my audition, and I was ready to pronounce Puccini with the best of them.

The program director greeted me. He took me into my first studio, sat me before a microphone and handed me a script.

It wasn't the script I'd studied.

It was a new one.

I was in big trouble.

This script had all new news items, new sports items, and a whole new set of unpronounceable names from the world of longhair music.

Well, let's just say I didn't turn this one over with the grace and ease of Tinker-to-Evers-to-Chance.

And when I was done stumbling and bumbling, the program director had a hard time disguising his glee.

"Thank you very much," he gloated. "You know what I suggest for you? Try to get a job on a small station. Get experience. In a year or two, call us back and we'll give you another audition. But you've got to get some experience."

He was kissing me off. And I just stuck out my cheek and took it. As he was showing me the door, I was thanking him profusely. But just as I was about to leave, I turned and asked him a question.

"Oh, by the way," I said. "What did Merle Jones think? What did Mr. Jones say?"

Well, he started giving me this line about how Merle Jones was a very busy man and couldn't be bothered with things like this and didn't really want to get involved . . . and suddenly I realized that Merle Jones had never heard one word of my audition.

Whatever it was that had made me send the letter to Merle Jones's home was triggered again. And once again it worked.

"Hey," I insisted, "wait a second. You heard him just the same way I did. Mr. Jones wanted to hear me *personally*."

The program director started giving me the brush-off again, the same speech.

"Look," I told him, "I'm not moving until I talk to Mr. Jones. Now, do you want to call him, or do you want *me* to call him?"

If looks could kill, I would have been dead and buried right there.

But the program director went to the telephone, called Jones, and explained what had occurred. I heard a few *uh-huhs* and a couple of *arghs* and then a nice, satisfying, "I'm sorry. Okay, I'm sorry, we'll do it right away."

So we returned to the studio and I did my audition again, this time with Merle Jones listening. I was a little better, but still wasn't reminding anyone of Lowell Thomas or Ed Murrow. When I was done, Merle Jones's voice came into the studio over the intercom, inviting me to come up to his office.

When I got there, he had a big grin on his face. "Sort of tough, huh?" he asked.

I immediately went into this song and dance about how I wanted to be a baseball announcer, how I wanted to tell people about the things I saw at the ballpark, the excitement and the great plays and the great players. "Do Puccini and Tchaikovsky and *La Bohème* and all that stuff have anything to do with baseball?" I asked.

He smiled again.

"Well, no," he said. "All I wanted to hear from you was your voice. And let me tell you something. You have an exciting timbre. You're like a Graham MacNamee or a Ted Husing. You could be exciting."

I was feeling pretty good about this time. MacNamee and Husing were two of the great names of radio sportscasting.

"Now it's up to you," he said. "I don't know if I can get you started for much money, but if you want to try, if you want to gamble, I'll get you a start. After that, you're on your own. Right?"

"Right!" I exclaimed.

About ten days later, I heard from a Bob Holt. He had been the chief announcer at KMOX, and he had just left to take over as the station manager at WCLS in Joliet, Illinois.

He was looking for a sports and special-events announcer. When he had mentioned that to his old boss, Merle Jones had told him about me. Jones hadn't told him that I didn't have any experience. He had just said I was young, hungry, and looking for a new job.

A couple of days later, I packed up my car and my wife and headed north for Joliet, Illinois.

I also decided, at Holt's suggestion, to change my name from "Carabina" to "Caray." It had a quicker sound, he said, and while my first reaction was negative, I decided, why not? I had no paternal relatives, I was starting a new job in a new town. So, I became—legally—Harry Caray. Forever.

RUNS **HITS** **CHAPTER**

0 0 5

Every once in a while these days, I'll run into someone who still says, "Hey, Harry, I remember you from Joliet, back when you were doing radio there in the forties."

Well, I sure as hell hope they don't remember it too well.

I'll admit I did have an exciting timbre in my voice. And absolutely, I knew sports, especially baseball. And, no question, I had all the enthusiasm and energy in the world.

But I definitely had to learn about my new profession— broadcasting.

Joliet is pretty much your basic midwestern city. It had some heavy industry at the time, a little shipping on the Des Plaines River, and it was a railroad center for the farmers in the area. The population these days is around eighty thousand; back then, it was probably a little more than half that.

I did mostly local events during my early days at WCLS. We

had a couple of high schools—Joliet Catholic and Joliet Township—and a junior college that had a pretty decent basketball team, as I recall. Those were the sports I covered. As for special events, the winter bowling league and the summer softball beer leagues fit the bill quite nicely.

It's too bad they didn't make tapes of radio broadcasts back in those days. Because if they did, my first effort for WCLS would be one of the all-time favorites on the "bloopers and blunders" shows that are so popular today.

Basically, I figured if they sent you to a ball game, you talked into a microphone and told everyone what you saw. If they had you working from a studio, you read from the script. How hard could it be?

I found out very quickly.

There was a bowling alley in town that was on my beat, primarily because one of the advertising salesmen was trying to sell it airtime. He figured that if we gave it some free publicity, they might come back and pay for more.

My first day of work was a Monday, and it just so happened that the night before some lucky fellow had bowled a perfect game, a 300. Our hustling salesman convinced me that it would be a big scoop if I interviewed this bowler.

Now it's important to stress here that I thought all broadcasters worked off scripts when they conducted interviews. It's also important to keep in mind that there is *nothing* more difficult in our business than reading from a script. If you don't believe me, take something that you've written—or better yet that someone else has written—and try to make it sound natural and conversational. Just about anybody can talk extemporaneously and not make a fool of himself on the radio. But the ability to read well on the air is the mark of a professional announcer.

As I was soon to learn, I was not yet a professional announcer.

After the interview with the bowler was set up, I spent all afternoon writing the script. Then, very carefully, I typed a copy for myself with a carbon for my interviewee.

Question 1: It must have been a big thrill bowling that 300 last night, wasn't it?

Answer 1: Oh, yes it was, Harry, it was the biggest thrill of my bowling career.

That's exactly the way I did it, right on down the line. First I wrote the question, and then I wrote the answer. Just the way I knew the big-timers did.

Shortly before we went on the air, I calmly handed the script to Mr. Perfect Game. He was just as green as I was. Either he didn't know enough or he was too shy to tell me that he could think up his own answers, thank you. I wish he had, because then at least one of us would have known what we were doing in that studio.

By the time the engineer gave me the signal that we were on the air, my hands were shaking. The script papers were rattling around and making so much noise that the few people listening to 250-watt WCLS probably thought a helicopter was landing in our studios.

The guy I was interviewing was in even worse shape. When he saw how frightened I was, he got twice as nervous. The way his hands started to shake and his papers started to rattle against the microphone, the folks at home—if any were still listening— probably assumed we were being invaded.

I didn't let it bother me, though. I just pressed valiantly ahead.

I asked the first question exactly the way it was written on my script.

"It must have been a big thrill . . . blah, blah, blah."

And Mr. Perfect Game rose to the occasion. He gave an excellent reading—of the answer to the fifth question.

"Yes, Harry, my wife's a terrific cook, but I probably owe it all to the hot dogs down at the alley. They give me all the energy I need to bowl those ten frames."

And so it went.

I'd ask the second question, he'd answer the third.

I'd ask the third question, he'd answer the first.

It was a disaster.

I was embarrassed afterward, but I wasn't ashamed. One thing I've learned: Everyone makes mistakes. You just have to learn from them—that's also part of being a professional.

I accepted the constructive criticism of my superiors, then the next day I went out and did a little better. And the day after that still better. Every day I improved a bit more. And every day I loved the job a *lot* more.

After three or four weeks of working, I was convinced I was a natural at this business. I began writing letters to larger stations, applying for jobs. These weren't brash letters like the one I had sent to Merle Jones—I knew better than that now. They were professional and serious.

After about a year and a half of diligently writing letters, one of those bigger stations replied and offered me a job. Once again I packed up my family and headed off, this time to Kalamazoo, Michigan.

I was going to be the sports director of WKZO, 590 on your AM dial.

As it turned out, WKZO was to broadcasting what Miami of Ohio was to football coaching. Miami of Ohio has produced coaches like Paul Brown, Woody Hayes, Ara Parseghian, John Pont, and Bo Schembechler. Well, WKZO has just about as impressive a list of success stories on its roster of alumni.

A few of us worked there at the same time in the early 1940's, ambitious kids struggling to make our way in an extremely competitive business.

Our patron, the owner of the station, was a man named John Fetzer. Using WKZO as a foundation, he built one of America's great broadcasting empires. Fetzer had founded the station in 1930 with a little wireless equipment, $156, and an eye, if I say so myself, for young talent. They say he survived the Depression by trading airtime for meal tickets.

By the time he started breaking up his empire—just within the past few years—he owned three other radio stations, four television stations, numerous Muzak and cable-TV franchises, a sports-television network, and the Detroit Tigers of the American League, which he sold to pizza magnate Tom Monaghan for a paltry $53 million a few years ago. Fetzer also was a regular on the Forbes 500, the exclusive list of the richest people in America, with a net worth conservatively estimated to be $160 million.

The news director for WKZO back in those days was a fellow named Paul Harvey. He had a booming voice and a distinctive cadence. And he had this way of making the most trivial thing seem to be as important as the bombing of Pearl Harbor— which, by the way, occurred while we were both working there.

I don't have to tell you that Paul has gone on to become the most successful radio broadcaster in history. "Hello, Americans . . . this is Paul Harvey . . . stand by for news." He has been using that sign-on for years. And the sign-off has never changed. From the first time I heard him in 1941, right up until today, Paul has used that unique and inimitable . . . "Good day."

Before I arrived in Kalamazoo, Paul had been doing some sportscasting, too. In fact, I have a photograph of him doing a football game in 1941, sitting next to his wife, Lynee, and his engineer, Carl Lee, who went on to become president of Fetzer Broadcasting Company.

Over the two years Paul and I worked at the station together, we developed strong feelings of mutual respect. We both knew, even then, that we were going places in this business, that it was just a matter of time.

Some of the other successes who started out at WKZO around the time I did were Roy Rowan, who became the CBS announcer for television shows like *I Love Lucy* and *Rawhide*, and Ralph Story, who also moved to Los Angeles, hosting a few quiz shows before becoming a TV news anchor out there. Even the guys behind the scenes did well for themselves. As I mentioned, Carl Lee, our engineer, became the president of Fetzer, and Hooper White, our continuity director, became executive vice-president of Leo Burnett, the giant international Chicago-based advertising agency. Later, Tom Snyder would work at the station, and so would Larry Osterman, who broadcasts the Tigers' games now.

The one thing we all had in common back in the 1940's was that we were hired by a fellow named Ray V. Hamilton. Ray had been brought in by Fetzer from ABC in Chicago to be general manager of the station.

Harvey had worked as special-events director for Hamilton at KXOK in St. Louis, and Ray loved Paul. He used to tell me that Paul was so good he could describe nonstop for an hour a parade that wasn't even parading—never stumble over a word.

The station was carrying the Tigers' radio network broadcasts, which featured Harry Heilmann, but Hamilton wanted to do a locally produced pregame and postgame show. Initially, my job was to do those shows, plus a daily sports report, and play-by-play for the football and basketball broadcasts of Western Michigan University, the local Kalamazoo college.

Then, one summer, Hamilton decided to my delight that plugging into the Tigers' network wasn't sufficient, that we should be doing baseball games of our own. So he sent me up to Battle Creek to do play-by-play of a big semipro tournament. A local team, Kalamazoo Sutherland Paper, was featured in the tournament. It was the first baseball play-by-play I had ever done. But I realized pretty quickly it wouldn't be the last.

We had not sold much commercial time—this was an experiment, remember—so between innings, my instructions were to ask the listeners to send in cards and letters if they wanted us to do more baseball. The response was overwhelmingly positive. Whatever I was saying, the people were enjoying it.

One of the things I did say during that tournament, by the way, was "It might be . . . it could be . . . it IS a home run!"

I don't remember who hit the home run. I don't remember the situation or the score. It wasn't anything I planned, it just came out—a natural description, a logical progression of thought.

Another thing I'm fairly certain I said during that tournament was "Holy cow!" People always want to know where that expression comes from. I'm not exactly sure, but I do know it's something I've been saying all my life. I've been told that Phil Rizzuto, the former great shortstop of the New York Yankees, has been credited for being the first to use that phrase on the air. I don't see how that's possible. Phil didn't become a broadcaster for the Yankees until after I'd started broadcasting for both the Browns and the Cardinals. Phil was still playing shortstop for the Yankees. If he was saying it, he was saying it only to Jerry Priddy, his second-base partner in the field. My guess is that I was the first to use it professionally on a broadcast of baseball, but it's no big deal.

To me, "Holy cow!" seemed like the right kind of exclamation. It was forceful, exciting, and certainly couldn't offend anybody. And, of course, more important than any of the above, it was the only exclamation I could come up with that didn't involve profanity. Don't forget my roots—kids on the street didn't go around saying "Holy cow!" when they got excited. But I couldn't say what they *did* say on the air.

Wherever it came from, it just seemed right to capture the excitement of a particular moment—a home run, a great catch, a spectacular throw.

It still does. And, funny thing, when I go a game or two without using it, I get mail wondering why. But to use it just to use it defeats the purpose. Then it becomes contrived, and the whole reason I started saying it was because it came naturally.

The years in Kalamazoo were good ones. I learned a lot about my profession there, but by 1943 I felt ready to move on. I wanted to move to a bigger station in a bigger city. Once again, I sent out tapes and résumés. I was certain someone would write back, offering a job.

I was right. Only, as usual, it didn't happen exactly the way I had planned.

The job offer came from an employer named Uncle Sam. The war effort was expanding. I had been reclassified and no longer had my deferment. Even with my lousy eyesight and my dependent family, I was 1-A.

I didn't know if that meant I was destined to fight the Germans in Europe or the Japanese in the Pacific, but I did know it meant I had better get Dorothy and Skip back to her parents' place. We would all have to be settled when I was summoned and sent off wherever to make the world safe for democracy.

So I quit my job in Kalamazoo, packed up the car once again, and headed down Route 66 for St. Louis.

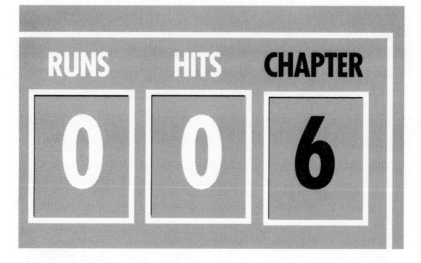

RUNS   HITS   **CHAPTER**

0   0   **6**

I was back in St. Louis so I could be on hand for my induction physical. When I was called, everything went along all right until I took off my glasses. My eyes are weak; I'm very myopic. I couldn't see the scoreboard at Sportsman's Park, let alone the eye chart across the room. So I was reclassified again, this time to 1-AL, which meant I was in the limited-service category. At that time, they weren't taking people in limited service, especially those who had a wife or children. That was the good news.

The bad news was that I was unemployed, and I still had a wife and son to support. So I went out to get a job. I thought about going back to Kalamazoo, but I was afraid that once I got there, I'd be reclassified *again,* and would have to come right back to St. Louis. So I knocked on the door of every radio station in St. Louis. I handed out résumés and auditioned for anyone who was willing to listen. I was trying to get a job as a sports announcer, but I would have done anything. I would have jumped at any opportunity. During the war years, not a lot of sports was being broadcast. So I wasn't being picky.

Finally, I landed a job as a staff announcer for station KXOK. Being a staff announcer means I did an eight-hour stint on the board, I handled my own microphone, I read the news, gave the station breaks, the time, and the weather. A far cry from my ideal job as a sports announcer—but beggars can't be choosers.

I was there for about three months, reading my announcements and biding my time. I was also constantly going in to my boss—the station manager, Chet Thomas—begging for the opportunity to do some sports.

Again, remember: luck and desire.

Jerry Burns was the man doing the nightly sports show. It so happens that right at that time, he was drafted. And my constant badgering of Chet Thomas paid off. He gave me the opportunity to do a fifteen-minute sports show at ten-fifteen every night.

I was determined to make the most of this opportunity.

Just as I had done in Joliet and Kalamazoo, I wrote my own material. I didn't take news off the wire as was the habit of most sports announcers in those days. I covered the town. I tried to pick up stories. I tried to break stories. I tried to get scoops. But while in Kalamazoo, I had been about the only game in town, there were a lot of quality sports announcers in St. Louis.

The city was the gateway to the West. It was major league and big time. There were many radio stations in town, and the competition to attract listeners was stiff. My competition came from people like France Laux, who for years did baseball with CBS. And Dizzy Dean, the great Cardinals' Hall-of-Famer. Johnny O'Hara, Ray Schmidt. And there were others. All with their own followings.

I knew if I wanted to attract an audience of my own, I had

to be different. Fortunately, it was easy for me to be that. What I did in St. Louis was exactly what I had done in smaller markets like Joliet and Kalamazoo. I was *myself.*

In those days, sportscasters pretty much just told you the scores, reported the trades, read you the schedule of games, and so forth. Occasionally, they even tore the stories off the United Press International or Associated Press wires and gave you a little breaking news. One broadcast seemed no different from the other. They were bland, bland, bland, not to mention boring, boring, boring.

I think it was simply the habit of the day. They took the easy way out.

My sports show was different. I criticized, I ripped, I offered opinions. Other radio announcers, particularly sports announcers, didn't. That stuff was reserved for the newspapers. They were the ones who were supposed to be controversial. They were the ones who were supposed to get the scoops. The newspaper guys didn't much care for radio people back then. They felt that they did the work, got the stories, and then those stories went out over the wire and some radio announcer could simply read the fruits of their labor on the air.

Well, I didn't want to be like that. I wanted to do the work and get my own stories, speak about my own opinions and observations. Howard Cosell has made a big deal about telling it like it is. Well, I was telling it like it is over forty years ago. That's the only way I knew how to do it. It's *still* the only way I know how to do it. It's also the way I like it.

By the way, I do think a lot of that antagonism on the part of the print reporters toward the radio and TV guys has subsided. For one thing, radio and TV announcers are now journalists, and we get more respect for being journalists. For another thing, there're a lot of crossovers. Newspaper reporters are often on television and radio. Television and radio broadcasters often have newspaper columns or write magazine pieces.

One of my first heroes was a crossover journalist: Walter Winchell. I read his columns religiously, and I loved his radio broadcasts. I don't know if I was Mr. or Mrs. America or all the ships at sea, but I certainly did tune in every night.

Walter Winchell may have been wrong, but he was never in doubt. You might not have agreed with him, but you always listened to him. His column was great newspapering, his show was even better radio. And his sources were good, too. Even his detractors had to admit that Winchell broke more than his share of big stories between his patented dots and dashes.

So in contrast to the dull, boring sports coverage that listeners were accustomed to, I set out to be the Walter Winchell of sports. Every night at ten-fifteen, I'd be on the air blasting, ripping, praising, and slashing. I would editorialize, and I would break real scoops. I'd tell the truth. I used—perhaps overused —stories from sources I described as unidentified and unimpeachable, another Winchell trademark.

Broadcasters had never before done things like that in St. Louis. They had always left that kind of work for the newspapermen, for the columnists and the beat writers from the *Globe-Democrat* and the *Post-Dispatch*.

It didn't take long before people were asking, "Who the hell is this Harry Caray?" The cards and letters were pouring into the station. The ratings were growing.

Frankly, the timing couldn't have been better. In St. Louis, baseball is king. And in 1944, St. Louis was the king of baseball. It was the only time in history that there was an all-St. Louis World Series.

For the Cardinals, it was no big deal. Three times in the 1930's, they had won the National League pennant. In 1942, they had won the World Series; in 1943, they had lost in five games to the New York Yankees. They were led by stars like Stan Musial and Marty Marion, the slick-fielding shortstop who hit .267 and was elected the league's Most Valuable Player.

For the Browns, though, this was a remarkable achievement, the only pennant they won in their half-century in St. Louis. Even against the unimposing wartime competition, it was damn near a miracle. The year before, the Browns had finished sixth in the eight-team American League, and that, eluding the basement, was something of a moral victory. Yet in '44—with more players who were 4-F—they managed to beat out the Detroit Tigers and the Yankees in a furious pennant race with a team that featured shortstop Vern Stephens (he was their big hitter, with a .293 batting average, 20 home runs, and 109 runs batted in), Jack Kramer, Denny Galehouse, and the aces of the pitching staff, Nels Potter and Sig Jakucki.

Then the Browns carried the Cardinals to six games before losing in a Series that was notable for one other thing besides featuring two teams who shared a little ballpark at the corner of Grand Boulevard and Dodier Street in a rundown residential neighborhood in St. Louis. The two clubs set a World Series record by striking out a combined ninety-two times in those six games.

Anyway, it was in this atmosphere—when sports interest was at an all-time high in St. Louis, when the people on the home front depended on the diversion of sports to help them forget the daily tragedies of the war reports, when even winning important battles required the most profound sacrifices—that I started to make a name for myself in St. Louis.

And once that started to happen, I started to pursue my ultimate goal, I started to focus on the objective that I thought represented the greatest success I could achieve in the business

—to broadcast baseball play-by-play in St. Louis. I didn't have a plan. I didn't have a timetable. But I knew exactly what I wanted.

I never thought that it would happen as quickly as it did.

It seems kind of quaint when you consider it from the perspective of today, but back in those days, four decades ago, when radio sportscasting was relatively young, baseball owners did not appreciate the commercial value of their product. Today, they make millions upon millions of dollars—more money even than they take in at the gate through ticket sales—selling exclusive radio and television licenses for their games. But back then, they practically gave it away. They thought the publicity was basically payment enough.

The way it worked was pretty simple.

A company consulted its advertising agency and decided the best way to sell its product was to reach a largely male audience. You did not do this by buying time on *Don McNeil's Breakfast Club.* You did it through sports. Represented by its advertising agency, the company then bought time from a radio station to broadcast ball games. At the same time, the company advised the ball club that they were interested in sponsoring broadcasts of its games over a particular radio station. They then paid a token fee for the rights, a pittance compared to what they're charged today. Chances were, if this was a city of any size at all, that more than one company and more than one radio station would be engaged in broadcasting ball games.

In 1944, in St. Louis, Missouri, in the inspiring wake of the all-St. Louis World Series, the latest company to reach this decision in consultation with its advertising agency was Griese-dieck Brothers Brewery, producers and purveyors of "Double-

Mellow" (I never did figure out exactly what that meant) Griesedieck Brothers light lager beer. Starting in 1945, Griesedieck
Brothers would, over radio station WIL, broadcast all home
games featuring the Cardinals and the Browns.

As I mentioned before, in cities with more than one team (St.
Louis, Philadelphia, Boston, New York, and Chicago), broadcasts of road games were allowed only with the other team's
permission. In St. Louis, given the depth of antipathy between
the two clubs—the Browns owned the ballpark, but the tenants,
the Cardinals, owned most of the fans' hearts, not to mention
an extraordinary record of success—such permission was almost
never granted.

Anyway, in the autumn of 1944, Griesedieck started to prepare for its plunge the following spring into baseball broadcasting. The way to prepare for this, they figured, was to spend the
winter broadcasting minor sports events—everything from college basketball to the American Hockey League, from boxing to
Ping-Pong to wrestling—to iron out the kinks and learn the fine
points of the business before baseball started.

And the man they hired to handle these insignificant broadcasts, the voice of St. Louis Flyers hockey (it was the first play-by-
play I ever did in St. Louis) was yours truly, Harry Caray,
reporting now over WIL, 1230 kilocycles on the AM dial.

When the brewery's advertising agency—Ruthrauff & Ryan
—hired me, it was with the understanding that I was going to
be strictly the number-three man. The young man of the future.
When baseball rolled around, they were going to hire a big-name
play-by-play man, and a former ballplayer to be his sidekick. I
would read the commercials, do a pregame show, a little postgame, the nightly sportscast, and play-by-play of the minor
sports. To me, it sounded great. The opportunity of a lifetime.

I wasn't yet twenty-five years old, and the world was opening up to me like an oyster.

After I had been working there a few months, they still had not hired a play-by-play man for baseball. They had hired a color analyst—Gabby Street, former Cardinal manager, former catcher of Walter Johnson with the Washington Senators, and the man who caught the first ball ever thrown off the Washington Monument. But they continued to fail in their attempts to lure a big national name, like Bob Elson from Chicago or Mel Allen or Red Barber from New York, to St. Louis.

Now here I am, working hard, doing a good job. They're tickled pink with me—but they're not even *considering* me as their baseball play-by-play announcer. It didn't make sense to me. They're raving about my style, but they won't give me the job I'd be best at! Time and again, I knocked on the door of Oscar Zahner, the agency vice-president who handled the Griesedieck account and had hired me, and explained to him that I was the answer to his problems.

"What do you need those guys for?" I would ask him. "You need something different. You need someone young and vital. You need *me.*"

Oscar seemed to appreciate my passion, even though he never did agree with my sentiment or buy my message. Every time, he would listen to me patiently and then explain that I was too young, that my time was coming, but that they needed someone with experience now. He told me that they had budgeted a significant amount of money (I was making $8,000 a year at the time; a significant amount of money was probably something like $25,000–$30,000 a year) to invest in a big name, and that was what they intended to do.

For some reason, I wouldn't take Oscar's no for an answer.

I'm not sure what the reason was—probably part of it was just a gut instinct. I had the same gut instinct when I wrote that letter and sent it to Merle Jones's home. I had the same gut instinct when I bugged Chet Thomas about my credentials as a sports-caster. It's the same gut instinct I've used during five decades in this business.

Yet I also had some support, some backup. You see, the *fans* liked me. People would come up to me in the street and ask if I was going to do baseball play-by-play. I was popular, and I could tell my popularity was growing. Sure it made me feel good. But it also made me think these guys at the station were crazy not to give me my shot.

Now it was getting late. By the last week of January, they still had not hired a play-by-play man. Spring training would begin in a matter of weeks, and time was running out. For them. And for me. They said they wanted me for the future—but I decided the future was now.

Who was it who said that authority is 20 percent given and 80 percent taken? I decided to exercise my 80 percent and find out if that was true. Without an appointment, without telling Oscar Zahner or anyone else from the advertising agency or the radio station what I planned to do, I went right to the top to sell myself. I drove out Gravois Avenue and paid a visit to Edward J. Griesedieck, the president of the brewery.

I knew this violated all the rules, I knew it was *verboten*, but since I had gone to work for him the previous fall, I had gotten to know Mr. Griesedieck. We'd have lunch periodically; he'd ask me about this guy or that guy. On a friendship basis, I felt comfortable going into his office for a chat. He was an affable man, democratic, not at all condescending despite his high station in life. So I had no qualms, and I didn't pussyfoot around when I went in to see him.

"Mr. Griesedieck," I said, "here it is the last week of January, and you still don't have a number-one baseball announcer. I've heard what everyone says, that you're looking for a big name to compete with Dizzy Dean and the rest of them, but I don't know why. For one thing, those guys you want are all tied up elsewhere. But for another thing, you need somebody fresh. Somebody new. You don't need Mel Allen or Bill Stern. And to tell you the truth, I don't think you'll get those guys. You know what's going to happen? You'll come up to spring training without an announcer, and you'll *have* to use me. But that'll be terrible, because by then everyone'll know I wasn't really your first choice." I just kept rattling on, not giving him a chance to cut me off. "What do I have to do to convince you, Mr. Griesedieck? You've heard me on basketball. You've heard me on boxing and on hockey. Don't you think I'm exciting?"

"Oh, Harry," he said. "Sure you're exciting. I wish I had your future. You're gonna be great." I knew what was coming. He was just like Oscar Zahner on this point. "But you're just too young."

I was starting to get excited. "What's the difference if I'm doing football or baseball?" I demanded. "If you think I'm worth paying to do the other sports, why won't you let me do baseball?"

And that's when he said something I'll never forget. Because it drove me right over the edge.

"To tell you the truth, Harry," he told me calmly, "when I'm listening to a baseball game, I like to listen to a guy like France Laux."

Well, France Laux was one of those announcers who had inspired me to write my letter to Merle Jones. I respected Laux a great deal, but you know how it is when you're young and frisky. You always figure you can be better than someone else, and I did feel that I could add another dimension to a baseball broadcast.

"What I like about him," he continued, "is that when I'm listening to him, I'm listening to a real pro. He calls every ball, every strike. I can have a cup of coffee and read my newspaper, and even though he doesn't miss a play, I don't have my concentration interrupted."

That was it! I couldn't sit there silently any longer. Mr. Griesedieck had started to make my point for me, and I was going to finish it.

I pounded my hand on his desk and started talking emphatically.

"Mr. Griesedieck, that's exactly what I was talking about when I walked in here!" I told him. "Can you read your newspaper while I'm announcing?"

"No," he said, a bit confused.

"Because I make you pay attention to the game, I don't *let* you read a newspaper! Yet here you are, spending hundreds of thousands of dollars to sponsor baseball, and when your commercial comes on, when your handpicked announcer is selling your product, you're busy reading the paper! You're wasting your money with that kind of announcer, Mr. Griesedieck. You need someone who's going to keep the fan interested in the game. Because if they're paying attention to the game, they'll pay attention to the commercial!"

When I was finished with my speech, the room was dead silent. An interminable length of time, a lifetime, seemed to go by. My career flashed before my eyes. I figured it was over. I'd gone too far. Why wasn't I content with waiting? Why did I have to be so pushy? Not only wouldn't I be doing baseball, I wouldn't be doing *anything.*

Mr. Griesedieck never took his eyes off my face all this time.

His eyes were riveted right into mine. And, looking at me all the time, he slowly reached for his telephone receiver. He never took his eyes off mine as he barked instructions to his secretary.

"Get me Oscar Zahner on the phone," he told her.

I was positive he was calling Zahner to tell him he'd just fired this brash young man—me. I was incredibly uncomfortable. And all the time he never stopped staring at me.

Then I heard him say, into the phone, "Oscar, I want you to come over here right away. It's very important." Oscar must have asked him why, because Edward J. Griesedieck then said, "I want you to meet your new number-one play-by-play announcer."

I almost fainted. I mean, I could barely comprehend it.

Then he hung up the phone. And now he had a big grin on his face. "You know," he said, "you're right. When I'm listening to a game, I never even *hear* the damn commercials. I must be crazy not to have thought of this myself!"

I was trying to stay calm, but I couldn't. Hell, I was jumping for joy. I was a one-man World Series celebration. Between laughs and whoops, I was thanking Mr. Griesedieck profusely. And he was laughing right along with me.

Finally, he asked me to quiet down. He said he had a plan. He wanted to have a little fun.

"Now, when Oscar comes in here, he's going to push that door open," Mr. Griesedieck said with an even bigger smile. "And when he does, I want you to be behind it so he doesn't see you. I want to surprise him. Because, you know, when he sees you, he's really going to squawk."

Not too much later, the secretary buzzed and said that Mr. Zahner had arrived. Mr. Griesedieck motioned to me, and I jumped behind the door.

Oscar Zahner was a little Napoleonic type of guy, about 5'6", with a tiny bristle of a moustache and a real brisk, all-business kind of walk. He was a great executive, and he was used to getting his way. He ran his office with an iron fist.

When he arrived at Mr. Griesedieck's office that afternoon—and he must have flown over, because he made it downtown from the ad agency to the brewery in record time—he opened the door, never saw me, and stormed up to Mr. Griesedieck's desk.

"What the hell do you mean, 'meet my new play-by-play man'?" he said. "You know we're talking to the biggest names in the business and we haven't made a deal with anybody yet." Oscar still hadn't noticed that I was standing behind the door.

"Oscar," Mr. Griesedieck told him, "relax, relax. I've got the perfect guy to do play-by-play."

Oscar was practically hopping up and down. "Who? Who?" he demanded.

"Turn around and meet him."

Oscar Zahner turned around. He saw me and began to scream. I really did think he was going to have a heart attack.

"Oh, no! No! No! Please! You can't do this to me!" Oscar said. He never stopped screaming. "We have too much money at stake! No! No! No! Ed, you can't do this to me."

I didn't say a word. It was one of the few times in my life I was actually speechless.

Mr. Griesedieck finally interceded and calmed Zahner down. He pulled rank, is what he did.

"Oscar, this is the way I'm going to go," he said. "This kid has a lot on the ball. He's different. He's fresh. Why should we go into this new endeavor with guys who have been talking about other beers, who have been with other sponsors?"

Then Mr. Griesedieck told Oscar about the talk we had just

had, and explained how my speech about the commercials had made an impact on him.

Finally, he gave Oscar an ultimatum.

"Oscar," he said, "I've made up my mind. I still sign the paychecks and I still select the ad agency. So you can accept this decision or you can resign as our agency."

Needless to say, Oscar Zahner did not resign the account.

This was in January. In April, Gabby and I started doing the games. By May, we'd really become a terrific baseball team. And people—the fans—were starting to realize it. We were fresh, we were different. We were starting to change the listening habits of St. Louis.

It was in May that I attended a luncheon, an Executive Club meeting. I'm in the back of the room, staying out of sight, as Oscar Zahner gave a speech. He didn't know I was there.

Sure enough, he's talking about the advertising business and some of the difficult decisions that have to be made, and he says, "Now, recently, we had a *very* tough decision to make. So many people thought that because we were going into a new venture like broadcasting major-league baseball, we should have a recognized name, a big name for our play-by-play announcer. But," he went on, "I didn't feel that way. I felt we needed something different, someone whose style would be in direct contrast to our competition. We needed someone who would have an impact on the audience. That's why, over a lot of protests and under much duress, I insisted on hiring Harry Caray!"

With that, I broke out laughing from my vantage point at the back of the room.

I think it was at that moment that I knew I'd made it in this business.

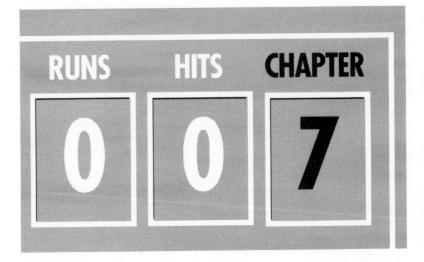

RUNS HITS CHAPTER

0 0 7

From the first exhibition game during that spring training, Gabby Street and I knew that we had something special going for us. We knew we were going to be one hell of a team.

Because of the war, the teams had not gone south to Florida to train. Instead, the two clubs shaped up just a couple of hours' drive from St. Louis. The Cardinals set up a camp in the Mississippi River town of Cairo, Illinois, while the Browns trained in Cape Girardeau, Missouri, another river town about twenty miles to the north of Cairo.

To get to know each other, Gabby and I would drive out to the camps together. Actually, I would drive, he would ride, and we would talk. For hours, we would talk. It didn't take me very long to understand why everyone called him Gabby.

He was born Charles Evard Street in Huntsville, Alabama, in 1882. I never once, in the seven seasons we worked together, heard anyone call him by his given name.

Gabby broke into big-league baseball in 1904, long before the Golden Age of Sports, long before Ruth and Gehrig and the rest of those great men whose bronze likenesses line the walls of the Hall of Fame made playing baseball a respectable profession. Now, being a ballplayer is as respectable as being a banker or a stockbroker. But there had been something slightly disreputable about playing baseball when Gabby Street did it, and he always reveled in that.

His first team was the Cincinnati Reds. He caught eleven games for them in 1904, played for both the Reds and the Boston Braves in 1905, catching a total of thirty-four games, and then returned to the major leagues with the Washington Senators. Gabby never hit much for Washington. His biggest season was 1911, when he batted .222, and his career batting average was .208. But he distinguished himself, nonetheless. Gabby was the brainy veteran catcher who turned a hard-throwing young man named Walter Johnson into a pitcher. In Gabby's first year with the Senators, Johnson, a green sophomore, was 14–14. In Gabby's final two seasons, Johnson was 50–30, and well on his way toward being the greatest right-handed pitcher in the history of the American League. The Senators showed their appreciation to Gabby by trading him to the New York Yankees. He played a season there, batted eighty-eight times, and retired from baseball.

The last of those eighty-eight at bats, however, was not his last appearance in the big leagues.

In 1930, after kicking around the bush leagues and coaching in the majors, Gabby Street was named manager of the St. Louis Cardinals. His first year on the job, the Cardinals won the National League pennant, though they lost the World Series in six games to Connie Mack's Philadelphia Athletics. His second year on the job, the Cardinals won 101 games and finished 13 games ahead of the second-place New York Giants in the National League standings.

Toward the end of the season, Gabby, who was almost forty-nine years old, rewarded himself by catching a couple of innings and taking an at bat. He grounded out. And then he went on to manage the Cardinals to victory over the Athletics in a seven-game World Series. The following year, however, the Cardinals finished sixth, and the year after that, with times hard, the team losing, and attendance declining, Street was replaced as manager by Frankie Frisch.

Now I've had a lot of partners up in the booth during my years of broadcasting baseball.

There was Jack Buck, a consummate professional and as fine a sports announcer as there is anywhere. Jack is in the broadcasters' wing of the baseball Hall of Fame in Cooperstown, New York, and deserves to be there.

There was Gus Mancuso, the former star catcher for the New York Giants. He took over on the Cardinal broadcasts after Gabby Street died, and did a terrific job.

Jimmy Piersall, a unique and intriguing character to this day, worked with me in Chicago. We really made it exciting while we were together with the White Sox.

And Joe Garagiola. His first job in broadcasting was as my partner in St. Louis. To this day, Joe is one of the best color men in the business.

Today, I work primarily with Steve Stone on the Cubs' telecasts. He's personable, young, articulate, a good analyst, and just terrific to be around in every way. I love the guy.

Dewayne Staats is the Cubs' main broadcaster on WGN Radio, and though he's very young, he's already had many years of major-league-baseball play-by-play experience. He will continue to get better. For the first several seasons with the Cubs,

I also worked with Lou Boudreau, a Hall-of-Famer if ever there was one. I admire him as a person and a partner.

Let me digress here for just a moment. You'll notice that quite a few names just mentioned are former players. I know that Howard Cosell has come out against the number of "jocks" in broadcasting booths these days. In some ways, he's got a point. There are a lot of fine young announcers around the country who aren't getting the exposure they deserve because of the networks' decision to hire ex-players. But on the other hand, a lot of those players are good broadcasters. They may be raw, but they can learn. I don't think they should put a jock in the booth just for the name value. But if he can do the job, why not let him talk for a living?

But let me get back to my partners. In particular, Gabby Street, because no partner I've ever had meant as much to me as he did.

When we first met, more than a generation separated us. But in spite of our age difference, we connected right away, almost instantly. We understood each other. I was young, I was inexperienced, but that never bothered Gabby, who had seen it all. He found it refreshing; he said it made him feel young again. I listened to Gabby and learned, and not only about baseball; I learned many of the most important lessons about life.

During our first couple of seasons together, Gabby and I established a ritual. I would pick him up at the Melbourne Hotel, where he lived, and drive him to the ballpark. We would do the game, and then, on the way home, we would stop for a ham sandwich and a beer. That's how the relationship really grew. That's where the confidences were developed. Not at the ballpark. Not at work. But away from the ballpark. Over a ham sandwich and a beer. That's when Gabby did his most important teaching. That's when I learned the most important lessons.

Gabby, you see, was old enough that he had already experienced most of the problems I had to look forward to.

By the time we hooked up, Gabby had been around the block many times.

He had much to do with the success of Walter Johnson. He won fame in a well-publicized stunt—catching the first ball thrown from the top of the Washington Monument (I don't know that there's ever been a second ball thrown off the Washington Monument; I can't imagine why anyone would want to do that again).

He served as an apprentice manager in the minor leagues, learning his trade all over again.

Then he went on to be the star manager of the World Champion St. Louis Cardinals.

Unfortunately, all of his life was not sweet. There was a lot of bitter, too. After being fired by the Cardinals, Gabby hit the depths. He drank too much. He lost his family. He lost it all.

But then he picked himself up by his bootstraps and rehabilitated himself. He established himself in Joplin, Missouri, married again, had wonderful children, and became the most respected citizen in the community. They named a wide boulevard for Gabby in Joplin. They just called it—what else?—Gabby Street.

By the time we became partners, Gabby also had some previous experience broadcasting baseball in St. Louis. But from the first day in spring training, when we made a tape of an exhibition game, when the only audience was an engineer, an executive, and maybe ourselves—we knew there was a special chemistry between us. It just felt right.

Gabby was the grizzled veteran. Everything that could happen in a baseball game he had personally experienced. He could explain every move, every nuance, every thought. He had neatly combed hair, a weathered face, and gnarled fingers. I've never met a catcher whose fingers weren't gnarled. Gabby himself used to tell the story that anytime two old catchers met and shook hands, you needed a plumber to separate them. Anyway, Gabby looked the part, and he was just terrific to work with and around.

Gabby combined this knowledge with a folksy, homespun-philosophical charm. You probably could compare him to Will Rogers. If you had to compare him to a contemporary sportscaster, Tim McCarver would be the closest. Gabby could explain everything perfectly, but he could also make you laugh. He was just a natural. But he was born forty or fifty years too soon. Today, he'd be making $5 million a year.

Where Gabby was wry, down-to-earth, and full of charming anecdotes, I was vibrant and youthfully enthusiastic. From 1945 right up until today, my style and philosophy as a broadcaster have not changed. Regardless of who signs my check, I have never felt I was working for a brewery, a ball club, or a station. I've always felt that my employer was the fan.

And I have always contended that if you put a microphone in front of anyone sitting in the bleachers and told him to start talking about the game he was watching, he would sound very much the way I do.

He might not use the same words. He might not have the experience, the professional veneer. But his voice patterns would be about the same.

He would be elated when I'm elated.

He would be depressed when I'm depressed.

He would be argumentative when I'm argumentative.

He would be complaining when I'm complaining.

He would question strategy and criticize umpires just the same way I do.

He would rip players for bonehead plays and congratulate them for great plays the way I do.

Sure, I always want the team I broadcast for to win. I wanted the Cardinals to win when I was doing their games. I wanted the Browns to win when I was doing theirs. I wanted the A's to win when I was broadcasting in Oakland. I wanted the White Sox to win when I was working for them in Chicago. And Lord knows how much I want the Cubs to win now.

It's not just my principle or philosophy to root for my home team. It's not even just an emotional attachment. In part, I'm being selfish. When the team you're broadcasting for wins, your audience is greater and your value increases.

Of course, that doesn't mean you have to make excuses for your team when they lose.

I've come under a lot of criticism in my day for being too hard on the hometown players. But I'll tell you something. When your star hitter comes up with the bases loaded and two outs in the bottom of the ninth and strikes out, there's no way to say, "And So-and-So just struck out to *win* the game." When your third baseman lets a ball go through his legs to let the winning run score, you can't say, "Well, the run scored, but it wasn't his fault."

As I said before, I've always believed in telling it like it is.

And in 1945, I told it like it was. Gabby spun his tales and taught the listeners about baseball—and we were off and running for the greater glory of the Griesedieck Brothers Brewery.

People began to talk about us. And about our beer.

There were two other broadcasts of the game in St. Louis at that time. Most prominent was the team of Dizzy Dean and Johnny O'Hara, representing Falstaff on the much more powerful station KWK. France Laux and his partner, Ray Schmidt, represented Hyde Park Brewery on KMOX, CBS's 50,000-clear-watt channel.

Honesty compels me to say that while Gabby Street and his little-known partner, Harry Caray, on WIL, were a poor third when we started, before it was all over we were the Silky Sullivan of the pack. We came up strong on the outside to win our audience, going away.

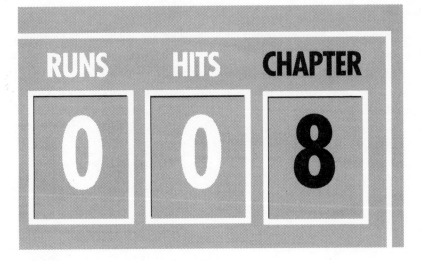

RUNS   HITS   CHAPTER

0   0   8

Nineteen forty-five was a pretty eventful year all around for the United States. The Germans surrendered. We bombed Hiroshima. The Japanese surrendered. Not bad for twelve months' work.

For the baseball fans of St. Louis, however, it was something of an anticlimax. Neither the Cardinals nor the Browns successfully defended the championships that had electrified the city just a year earlier.

After losing Stan Musial to the army, the Cardinals failed to win their fourth consecutive National League pennant. They gave it a run, but they finished second, three games behind the Chicago Cubs. The Cubs would not finish first again until 1984. By then, of course, I was broadcasting their games.

And the 1945 Browns finished third, six games behind the Detroit Tigers. They would not win an American League pennant again until 1966, long after they had moved to Baltimore and become the Orioles.

Day by day, week by week, month by month, Gabby and I were chipping away at the popularity of the opposition. However, because the teams we were covering were not winners, we didn't have the kind of impact I'd been hoping for. It's hard to *really* stir up enthusiasm in the fans when their team is out of the pennant race. If the Cards or Browns had been near the top of the first division, if there had been true baseball fever in the air, I'm convinced we would have caught, even surpassed, the other announcers in the audience ratings.

I am certain that would have been the case, because that is precisely what happened the next year in 1946.

All the great players returned from the war in 1946. So it was that the Browns also returned to their accustomed place in the second division, finishing a miserable thirty-eight games behind the pennant-winning Boston Red Sox. So it was, too, that the Cardinals were rejuvenated by the return of Musial and Enos Slaughter, Terry Moore and Howie Pollett and Murray Dickson. And so it was that the Cardinals engaged the Brooklyn Dodgers in a furious pennant race that season, a race that wasn't even decided on the final day. For after 154 games had been played, the two teams were dead even. Each had won ninety-six games. For the first time in major-league-baseball history, it would take an unscheduled play-off to determine a pennant winner. The Cardinals, of course, won. Pollett beat the Dodgers 4–2 in St. Louis in the first game, and two days later they closed out the Dodgers, 8–4, in Brooklyn's Ebbets Field.

It was during that pennant race that Gabby and I got our big break. Because interest in the Cardinals was so high, the brewery decided that when they were on the road and the Browns were idle or rained out, we could recreate away games from the information transmitted over the Western Union ticker.

The technique of recreating games was commonplace in those

days. In fact, a fellow by the name of Dutch Reagan built his reputation as a sports announcer for WHO in Des Moines by recreating Cubs games from the ticker back in the 1930's.

Which reminds me . . .

I never heard Reagan when he was broadcasting baseball in Des Moines, but I do know for a fact that he was a damn good sportscaster. I know this because, as I mentioned earlier, I worked with him. This was when Reagan was on the road promoting *The Winning Team*, in which he played the great Hall of Fame pitcher Grover Cleveland "Pete" Alexander, and costarred with Doris Day.

The studio sent Reagan to St. Louis because one of Alexander's great accomplishments—in the twilight of his long and illustrious career—occurred there. In the seventh inning of the seventh game of the 1926 World Series, the score 3–2 and the bases loaded, old Pete came in from the bullpen to strike out Tony "Poosh 'Em Up" Lazzeri, the second baseman of the New York Yankees.

The story of how that happened is part of the lore of the game in St. Louis, a legend still recounted in saloons by old-timers and younger guys—the ones about *my* age. According to the legend, there were two outs and the bases were loaded when Rogers Hornsby, the Cardinals' player-manager, brought in Alexander, who had already won the second and sixth games. Hornsby handed the ball to Alexander, reviewed the game situation, and then asked an essential question.

"Pete," Hornsby said, "I just want to know. Are you sober?" At this point in his career, Hornsby knew, Alexander was never sober, except on days when he was scheduled to be the starting pitcher.

"No, I'm not sober," Alexander replied, according to the legend. "But I sure as hell can strike this guy out anyway."

And, of course, he did.

When Reagan came into the booth, we reviewed that story, and we talked a little about the movie. This was between innings. When the next inning was about to start, I turned to him.

"You know," I said, "I've heard you were a pretty good broadcaster back in Des Moines. You're probably a bit rusty, but how would you like to do a little play-by-play?"

He said he would *love* to, so we worked together for an inning. I pointed to the names of the players on the scorecard while he called the balls and strikes and described the action. You could tell he had done it before; he was very professional.

Now I'll let you in on a little secret:

I don't discuss politics in public—although I might argue all night in private—but I will say that both times I had the opportunity to vote for Ronald Reagan as president, I did. I find him an impressive and sincere individual, and, besides, he's a former baseball announcer. How often will you get a chance to vote for somebody who used to broadcast baseball games? That's not such a bad reason, is it?

Anyway, back to St. Louis in 1946 . . .

When we started to recreate games off the Western Union ticker for the fans in St. Louis—fans who had two teams but who heard only home games—it was a novelty, a treat.

It turned out that Gabby and I had a kind of flair for it. We had a great capacity to improvise, which, when you're recreating a baseball game while in the confines of a studio, is unquestionably your most important asset.

One of the things that helped me was that I had recreated Cubs and White Sox games when I was working in Joliet. I'd done it a little differently, though. I condensed each game into a half-hour broadcast. I did the same thing in Kalamazoo. They'd give me the ticker tape for the whole game, then I'd take the scoring highlights and give them as much color, flavor, and authenticity as I could.

When something was brewing, I'd recreate each pitch. I'd build an inning and then maybe do something like, "Here's the two-two to Andy Pafko. He swings. It's way back! It might be . . . it could be . . . it IS . . . a home run!" Then I might follow that with, "During the sixth and seventh innings, neither the Cubs nor Cardinals threatened. Now, to the top of the eighth . . ."

At the beginning and the end of each one of those broadcasts, we announced that it was a recreation, that we were working off of information being transmitted to us over a Western Union ticker. But once we were into it, the fantasy was never interrupted. We would never even hint that we were in a studio in downtown St. Louis while the game was being played in Brooklyn's Ebbets Field or the Polo Grounds in Manhattan or Crosley Field in Cincinnati or Forbes Field in Pittsburgh. In fact, people used to argue all the time whether we were recreating a game or doing it live. Even to this day, people aren't sure.

Our big competition for the listening audience in St. Louis was the team of Dizzy Dean and Johnny O'Hara. Diz was a living legend, and justifiably so. He was a big, lovable country boy from the small town of Lucas, Arkansas. Dizzy could fracture the English language and the opposition's bats with compelling ease and zeal. In his six full seasons with the Cardinals—between 1932 and 1937—Dizzy chalked up 134 of his career victories, while losing just 78 times. He led the league in strikeouts four straight years, and in 1934, when the Cardinals won the World Series, his record was 30-7.

But as legendary and colorful as he was, Diz just never mastered the art of recreating ball games from the wire. I think he was bored with it.

The key to working the wire was imagination, employing a little poetic license. To be able to do this was absolutely essential.

For one thing, the information transmitted on the wire was minimal—B1, S1, B2, S2, 1BLF. That's ball one, strike one, ball two, strike two, single to left field. As the announcer, you had to supply the detail. You had to describe the batter digging in and stepping out of the box, the umpire calling time, the runner leading off first, the pitcher looking in for the signs, rubbing up the ball, and stepping off the rubber. You had to shade the outfielders to right and put the infielders at double-play depth. You had to invent the third-base coach calling for a conference to discuss the signs. And you had to use this license, this imagination, without altering the basic facts of the game. Because if you tampered with the facts, everyone would know it the next day when they read the accounts of the game written for the newspapers by the beat reporters who were traveling with the team.

So a foul ball for a strike became something like: "A high foul ball back to the railing behind the plate, the catcher is racing back, he's to the barrier, he reaches in, he . . . *can't* quite get it, and—holy cow!—a beautiful blonde in a red dress, amply endowed, makes a heck of a catch and has herself a souvenir."

For one thing, the machines broke down or slowed down all the time. The technology was relatively new, and its performance was uncertain. Eight or nine times every game, without fail, we would be sitting in the studio without receiving any information for two, three, four minutes at a time.

When that happened, I would provoke an argument down on

the field or maybe a disturbance in the stands that slowed play, or I would have a sandstorm kick up and have the players request time out to wipe their faces. Maybe, if there were two strikes on him already, I would have Musial foul off a few pitches. And then Gabby would chime in with his analysis of Musial's swing, and he would explain what a great, disciplined hitter Stan was. And to keep things going, I would play the devil's advocate just a little bit and I would say, "But Musial doesn't have the career batting average that Ted Williams has chalked up." And Gabby would explain that that was because Stan was the consummate team player—he would swing at the pitch an inch or two off the plate and try to get the hit that would win the game in a situation where a walk would not have any impact on the outcome—while Williams, Gabby would say, was so disciplined and so rigid and so concerned with his batting average that he would take the pitch, walk, and wind up stranded on first while the fellow batting after him made the last out of the game and the Red Sox lost.

In the context of the game, Gabby and I were talking baseball and making it fun and informative for the audience. We tried to keep the flow of the game intact, as if we were really there, and we developed a real sense of timing, of broadcasting give-and-take.

Over on KWK, meanwhile, Dizzy, who was working off the very same wire account, who would be stalled at precisely the same time that we were, filled the downtime by singing "The Wabash Cannonball." Every time the wire would go down, he would sing that same song. The fans loved it—at first. Now you might love chocolate ice cream, too—but after several quarts, you might get a little sick.

The people turned to me and Gabby. When a pennant race

gets close, fans don't want comedy and singing. They want *baseball.* And that's what we gave them.

As each week passed, we got bigger and bigger.

The only thing that marred our season is that Gabby and I didn't get to work the World Series. The Mutual Network had its own broadcasters.

It turned out to be a great Series. Which was a good thing, because it was the last for the Cardinals until 1964.

The Cards eventually beat the Red Sox in seven games. Enos Slaughter—who played the last two games with a broken elbow after being hit by a pitch in game five—scored the winning run in the bottom of the eighth of the last game when he came all the way around from first on a single by Harry Walker to break a 3–3 tie.

Slaughter broke with the pitch, and Walker lined the ball to left center. The Boston outfielder, Leon Culberson, scooped the ball up. Slaughter was already rounding second and was on his way to third. Culberson threw the ball to the shortstop, Johnny Pesky, while the place was going crazy.

Now, the third-base coach for the Cardinals was a guy named Mike Gonzalez, a Cuban who spoke broken English. As Slaughter heads to third, Gonzalez is yelling, "No! No! No!"—meaning, "Don't try for home!" Slaughter, thinking he was saying, "Go! Go! Go!," did just that. He tried to score. Well, Pesky was so shocked, he hesitated before throwing the ball. And that hesitation was what enabled Slaughter to score and win the Series.

It was a Series for the ages, but the Mutual Network broadcast came in for quite a bit of criticism.

Consider, if you will, the review from *Variety,* dated October 26, 1946.

The headline, in all capital letters, read:

NO HITS, NO RUNS, ALL ERRORS

The subhead read:

BASEBALL GAB
ALL TIME LOW

The review read, in part:

The World Series is over, but as far as radio is concerned, the
sour taste lingers on. It's been a long time since anything so
roused the industry as reaction to the alleged play-by-play accounts of the World Series games in Boston and St. Louis. . . .
    The beefs registered against the performances of announcers
Jim Britt from Boston, and Washington's Arch McDonald make
the meat shortage sound like a rumor. [Don't you just love the
way they write in *Variety?*] Thousands of squawks by wire, post-
card, letter and phone calls thundered into network headquarters and individual stations complaining about the sub-par work
of the announcers. Even the Mayor and city fathers of St. Louis
telegraphed a squawk!

So it went. In *The Sporting News* of the same date, it was
reported that there were so many complaints about the World
Series radio coverage that baseball was going to do a listener
survey and change the procedure for selecting World Series
announcers the following year.

Criticism of the broadcasts was particularly evident in St.
Louis, *The Sporting News* wrote, "where fans had listened all
season to the colorful descriptions of Dizzy Dean, Johnny
O'Hara, Harry Caray and Gabby Street. . . ."

Well, the survey was done and the system was changed. For

a couple of decades after the debacle of 1946, World Series broadcasts and—when television replaced radio as the principal means of reporting the play-by-play—telecasts featured an announcer of the Series participant that was playing host to the day's game.

This practice was discontinued in the 1970's, and I think the telecasts have lost something since. I mean, when the Cardinals were playing home games in the Series in 1985, I wanted to hear what Jack Buck had to say. And when the Tigers were playing at home the year before, I wanted to listen to Ernie Harwell. And when the Cubs make it this year, I want to be in the booth in Wrigley Field telling that national television audience exactly what this means to Chicago. It would add a hell of a lot to the telecast.

For all the interest Gabby and I stirred up in the Cardinals when we were recreating games, for all the uproar over our absence from the radio booth during the World Series, for all the fun we had at the old ballpark that summer, our biggest break may have occurred on the Sunday night the regular season ended. It happened in a restaurant up in the Hill.

There was a testimonial dinner honoring Joe Garagiola scheduled that night at a place called Ruggeri's. It went on even though the season ended in a tie, and the Dodgers were then on their way into town for the play-off. About a thousand people were in attendance that night. Among them were Gabby and I, who were seated at one table, and France Laux and his partner, who were seated at another.

The late Biggie Garagnani, who was Stan Musial's partner in the restaurant business, was the master of ceremonies. He was nice enough to introduce Gabby and me and Laux and his partner to the crowd, and then he went on with his regular program, which featured a few of the ballplayers, Dizzy Dean, Johnny O'Hara, and a fellow by the name of J. Roy Stockton, who was the sports editor of the *Post-Dispatch*.

Stockton's presence as an honored guest and featured speaker was most curious. While he was an important mover and shaker in the sporting scene in St. Louis, he was also a bitter and eternally angry enemy of the Cardinals' owner, Sam Breadon, who was there to see his team honored that night.

The wine flowed freely. I don't know if it was the booze talking or if Stockton's hatred for Breadon had just boiled over into a frothing and awful rage, but when he spoke, Stockton ripped into Breadon with a vicious relentlessness.

Noting that the Cardinals, by losing to the Cubs that day, had fallen into a play-off tie with the Dodgers, Stockton told the crowd that there was one person not bothered by the thought of the required play-off. That person was Sam Breadon. He inflamed the crowd by saying that Sam Breadon was delighted because now, through the play-off, he would be able to squeeze a few more bucks out of the season. Then Stockton reminded the crowd that Breadon had traded some veteran Cardinal stars that year like catcher Walker Cooper (to the New York Giants) and outfielder/first baseman Johnny Hopp and pitcher Mort Cooper (to the Boston Braves) to make sure that the team, while it remained good and competitive, would not be so strong that it would win the National League pennant without a race—and thus draw less at the gate. He went on like that for ten or fifteen embarrassing minutes.

When he finished, he was greeted by almost total silence. The speech had been totally inappropriate. We were there to honor a team that had won ninety-six games, to encourage them to win six more. There was a lot to cheer about. And, after all, it was to be a convivial evening, not one to display rancor.

The only thing Stockton said that had any truth to it was that the Cardinals had had a big year at the gate. They had, in fact, attracted 1,062,553 spectators to Sportsman's Park, the first time in the history of the franchise that they drew over a million.

Anyway, as Stockton was making his way through the silence back to his seat on the dais, someone stood up in the back of the room and yelled, "Harry Caray!" Then someone else stood up and said, "Hey, yeah, let's hear Harry Caray!" Then it started to mushroom. People started chanting for me. They had already heard from Dean and O'Hara, from a few players, from Stockton, and a few other dignitaries. Now, prompted by Stockton's unfair remarks, they wanted to hear from me. So Biggie called me up to the podium.

I've made a career out of avoiding the rubber-chicken circuit. I know I'm not a great after-dinner speaker, because I'm not a real good jokebook comic. I just can't tell the same stories over and over again to different audiences with verve and humor, the way fellows like Tommy Lasorda and Tim McCarver and Joe Garagiola do. But I am certainly glad the people in the room prevailed on me to speak that night. For as I made my way to the podium, people were patting me on the back and encouraging me. If I heard someone say, "Give 'em hell, Harry" one time, I heard it two dozen times.

But I didn't give them hell. I didn't even mention what Stockton had said. I didn't go up there firing away. I just gave them a little speech from the heart.

I talked about how fortunate the Cardinal player was. How being a Cardinal was almost tantamount to being guaranteed a World Series check every year. I mentioned how Sam Breadon —who was one of those Irishmen who wanted all his attributes to be kept a secret—did so many generous things for the community and for his employees that he would never permit to be publicized. I told how Breadon had kept Pete Alexander, who was an alcoholic, on the payroll for years, sending him a check every month even though he knew Alexander wasn't in shape to do any work. I talked about how if any other ballplayer ran into personal problems, Sam Breadon was always there to help him out.

When I finished, there was a big round of applause. As I left the platform, many in the crowd congratulated me. But Stockton gave me a cold stare. I knew I had made a mortal enemy.

And then Breadon pushed his way through the people to get to me. He stuck out his hand to shake and looked me straight in the eye.

"Young man," he said, "that was awfully nice of you. I will never forget it. And I really appreciate it."

Little did I realize how prophetic those words were to be. I had cast my bread upon the waters. And without my knowing it, the return would be greater than I ever could have expected.

During that off-season, Gabby and I did a weekly Hot Stove League radio program about baseball. The idea was to keep interest up—in the game of baseball, but also in us. The show was pretty popular, and in December the brewery figured it would be a good idea to send me to the winter meetings (baseball's annual off-season convention and swap meet where all the gossip and trading take place) in Los Angeles so I could file daily reports.

Nothing momentous happened at those meetings, but on the way back, whom should I run into on the airplane but Sam Breadon?

I greeted him with a series of questions, trying to get as much information as I could. He told me that the Pirates had tried to get Marty Marion, but that they hadn't offered anything worthwhile in exchange. The Dodgers, too, had talked trade, but nothing much had developed there, either. He invited me to sit with him, which I did.

"Oh, by the way," he said offhandedly after we were seated, "there *is* something you ought to be interested in. You know the rule that we can't broadcast our road games if the Browns are playing at home?"

"Yes." I nodded.

"Well, we had the good sense to get rid of that rule. We're free to sell our broadcasts—home and away—to anyone we want."

He paused for a minute, but I didn't say anything. So Breadon continued. It was indicative of his sense of fair play that he was already concerned about the Browns.

"I know when we go head-to-head, everyone in town will be listening to the Cardinals. That's why," he went on, "I won't sell our games until I'm sure there's another outlet for the Browns. I don't want to run them out of town."

He paused, but again I said nothing. Looking intently at me, Breadon then said, "I suggest you tell your people at the brewery about this. Because if there is a station available for the Browns, we will definitely sell both our home and away games."

As soon as I got back to St. Louis, I broke the news to the people at the Griesedieck Brothers Brewery. Everyone—all of us at the brewery, the Browns, the newspapers—assumed that the Cards would go with Falstaff and KWK because of Dizzy Dean. We were prepared for it. We weren't happy, but we were prepared.

A couple of months passed and Breadon didn't make a decision. Then, one day, he called me and invited me out to his office at the ballpark.

HARRY CARAY

After the usual pleasantries, he got down to business.

"You know, I have to make a heck of a decision," he began. "I've done a lot of soul-searching. You and Gabby have done a great job. So has Griesedieck Brothers. You've put together a nice little network. But you know, Falstaff tells me we'll have five times the network if they sponsor our games. They've got Dizzy and they're willing to pay a lot more money for the rights than I think Griesedieck Brothers can afford to pay."

I felt like a guy on death row who had just finished his last meal. I appreciated the fact that he was telling me his decision in person, but I wished he would just get the bad news over with.

"I've been doing a lot of thinking," he went on. "And I wanted you to be the first one to know the conclusion I've come to. I think that you and Gabby have done the best job for the St. Louis Cardinals. Dizzy Dean, on the other hand has done the best job for Dizzy Dean. My main concern is the Cardinals. That's why I want you to go down and tell your people at the brewery that, if they want them, Griesedieck Brothers can have the Cardinal games—home *and* away next season."

It took a few seconds for this to sink in. I'd been expecting a nice little kiss-off. When it *did* sink in, I was damn near speechless. I couldn't get out of my chair.

"Aren't you going to tell the people at the brewery?" he wanted to know.

"Right. Right," I muttered. Still dazed, I got up, shook his hand, and headed for the door. But before I could leave, he tapped me on the shoulder. When I turned around, he looked me straight in the eye.

"Young man, a few months ago at that testimonial dinner, I told you that I would never forget what you did. Well, consider this a proof of that."

Once again, my friends, luck and desire. Success in life depends so much on these. Little did I dream when I cast my bread upon those waters that it would come back to me in this form.

I had fulfilled a lifelong dream.

The voice of the St. Louis Cardinals, me, the little orphan kid from the wrong side of the tracks!

I couldn't believe it.

But it was true.

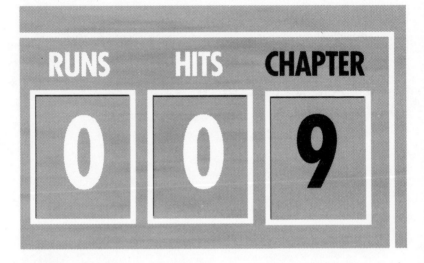

RUNS   HITS   CHAPTER

0   0   9

What a difference it was to actually be out on the road with the team. I no longer had to rely on my imagination and the ticker tape to broadcast road games. I was *there.* Traveling with the players, visiting parks I'd seen only in photographs.

I knew the Cardinal players, of course, just from announcing their home games. But I got to know them a little better, a little more intimately, by being with them away from home. In St. Louis, after a game, the players went home to their wives and children if they were family men; if they were single, they still went their separate ways when not at the ballpark. The team didn't pay your daily expenses when you were home, only when you were traveling. So, on the road, players were a lot more willing to gather in restaurants or bars.

Not surprisingly, one thing I had reinforced was my awareness that baseball players did not eat only their Wheaties for breakfast and milk and cookies for snacks. Ballplayers are young, healthy, normal people. They had then and they have now the same likes and desires and appetites for various things that I do. And that *you* probably do, too. I realized that the only difference between me and the ballplayers was that they had a unique and mostly God-given talent to play a game in a superior fashion than anyone else could play it.

Back in my early days on the road, I saw a lot of drinking. And I saw a lot of carousing. One thing I didn't see or hear anything about was drugs—except for the occasional "greenie," a stimulant that's a baseball way of life.

Now, I get pretty steamed up when people talk about alcohol and drugs in the same breath. They're not the same thing at all! Drugs are illegal! That's all there is to it. Last time I looked, alcohol was as legal as working for IBM. I take great exception to anyone trying to put alcohol and cocaine in the same category. When I was a young broadcaster, I never heard the word cocaine. It was strictly booze and broads.

In 1947, my first year on the road, I didn't particularly object to the booze-and-broads life-style, either. Now, to be honest about it, people talk pretty often about my life-style. As for the supposed womanizing, obviously it's a myth. I'm married, *very* happily, to Dutchie. And since my illness in 1987, I've realized that I'm not quite as indestructible as I thought I was. I still have my Budweisers, but I just take a little better care of myself than before. It used to be luck and desire, right? Now, it's luck and desire and moderation.

Anyway, I found traveling with the Cardinals to be an exciting development in my life. My love for the game was so strong, it was really a thrill for me to see some of the legendary ballparks around the country.

The Polo Grounds, where the New York Giants used to play, was a unique ballpark. It was 279 feet or so down the left-field line. Down the right-field line, I think it was only about 257 feet. But then, to show you the oddity of the park, center field was the biggest in the major leagues. It was about 450 feet straightaway. Weak hitters could hit cheap home runs in the Polo Grounds, while the good hitters, the power hitters, tended to suffer.

Ebbets Field in Brooklyn was vibrant, exciting, intimate. Today, the closest thing we have to that wonderful park is Wrigley Field. There's no doubt that the Dodgers are richer financially because of their move to Los Angeles, but baseball misses those little bandboxes like Ebbets Field. Too many of the new facilities are stereotyped, sterile. They all look the same. None has a particular flavor.

Some of the most thrilling games today are played in Wrigley Field and Fenway Park in Boston. It was that way at Ebbets Field. A team was never out of the game there. You couldn't relax with a ten-run lead. Anyone could put together a couple of hits, a couple of walks, a cheap home run or two and, wham, eight or nine runs were on the scoreboard before you knew it.

I'll never forget one game in Ebbets Field, the Cardinals were leading the Dodgers, and Howie Pollet was pitching. The game was almost rained out a number of times, but Brooklyn fans were sturdy. They didn't care too much about the bad weather. But when the fifth inning was over and the Cardinals were ahead 8–0, we figured the umps had to call it for sure. It was an official game at that point, and they didn't have to return any money to the fans. However, the umpires let the game continue. The Dodgers got four runs in the eighth—it was really pouring by that time—and we knew they'd never call the game. We had to play the final inning.

And, of course, the Dodgers made a typical Ebbets Field comeback. In the bottom of the ninth, they got a walk, a freak hit, then another weak hit along the infield, where the pitcher slipped and fell and couldn't get to the ball. All of a sudden, the bases were loaded with nobody out. This is when Tommy Glavianno was playing third base for the Cards. The next two balls were hit right at Tommy. The first went through his legs—two runs scored. It's now 8–6. The next one was a surefire double play. But Tommy's throw to second base went into right field. Another run scored. Men on second and third and it's an 8–7 ball game. Roy Campanella was the batter, and the Cards brought in a right-handed pitcher to pitch to him. He walked Campanella to fill the bases. That brought up Furillo, who lined a single to right, and the game was over. The Dodgers won 9–8. A typical Ebbets Field game.

The old St. Louis ballpark was the same kind of stadium. Small, intimate. It was called Sportsman's Park then, later to become Busch Stadium.

There was no Astroturf back in those days, which was fine with me. I don't like synthetic turf. I like grass. And you know what? I like the day games they usually play at Wrigley Field—and have for years and years—better than those six night games they played during the 1988 season. To me, Wrigley Field in the sunshine is the perfect ballpark under the perfect conditions. The green grass, the ivy-clad walls, the intimacy. It's wonderful. The fans in the stands can practically see the expression on every player's face. The Cubs televise every home game for free and still draw 2.5 million people to the park each season. How many more will lights draw for you?

Yet the lights were up in 1988 for the first time ever, and I have no doubt it all started when the Cubs made the National League play-offs in 1984. The Cubs had to play their two home games against the San Diego Padres in the afternoon—away from prime time, when there are more advertising dollars. After that, the commissioner of baseball stated that when the Cubs next win their division, they'd either have to have lights or they'd have to play their "home" games at some park other than Wrigley Field. How's that for a slap in the face of the fans? The Tribune Company, which owns the Cubs, really had no other choice.

I don't think the owners are too concerned about the fans. Of course, I don't think the owners, for the most part, are especially smart. Look at what's gone on with salaries the last ten or twelve years. The owners are crying poor. But who forced them to pay players all that money? Nobody. Who put a gun to their heads and said, "You've got to give Joe Blow two million bucks a year"? Nobody. I'd like to see these owners run their real businesses that way. If they had, they'd never have made enough money to buy a ball team in the first place. You think they'd pay a mediocre worker six hundred thousand dollars a year? Would they guarantee a fringe employee's salary for five years? No way. They'd be out of business. And they'd have nobody to blame but themselves.

I guess it sounds as if I'm a little nostalgic for some of baseball's old ways. That's partly true, I suppose, though I love the game today as much as I ever did.

There's one thing about the game that I don't miss. And it's something that I think people have forgotten about. Baseball used to be a segregated game. There were no black players in major-league baseball. Not until 1947, my first year on the road. That year, 1947, was the year baseball started to change America.

That year, 1947, was the year of Jackie Robinson.

Today, when there is no activity in American life as thoroughly integrated as sports, what happened in 1947 might not seem like much. But when it occurred, when Jackie Robinson broke the color barrier, it was a momentous event. It was earth-shaking. And nowhere did the earth shake as much as it did in St. Louis, Missouri.

Missouri was not one of the eleven states that joined the Confederacy in the Civil War. It was, rather, a border state that, like Kentucky and Maryland, remained in the Union while also remaining home to many who sympathized with Confederate goals. Yet in 1947, St. Louis, the state's largest city, was still very much a Southern town. Blacks did not necessarily have to sit in the back of the bus or drink from a separate water fountain, but it was clearly still a segregated place. In Sportsman's Park, for instance, most of the black customers sat in the right-field pavilion as a matter of habit.

And the ball club reflected the city. The Cardinals had for the most part always been a team of big old Southern farmboys, and the 1947 edition was no different.

Marty Marion, the great shortstop whose exclusion from the Hall of Fame is a travesty, hailed from South Carolina. Terry Moore was from Alabama. Enos Slaughter is ever the son of North Carolina.

A story developed that some of the Cardinals (many suspected the Southern contingent) attempted to lead a players' strike against Robinson the first time the Cardinals and Dodgers were scheduled to play that fateful season. According to the story—which was reported after the fact by Stanley Woodward, the legendary sports editor of the *New York Herald-Tribune*—Sam Breadon advised Ford Frick, the National League president, that the strike was being plotted, and Frick advised Breadon that the league stood firmly behind Robinson and that any strikers would be summarily suspended. Later, many Cardinal players would deny that any such strike was ever contemplated, while others admitted that there had been some discussion of it. But the fact is that on May 6, 1947, as scheduled, the Cardinals went into Ebbets Field and lost to the Dodgers pretty much without incident. Which was about how things went that year. The Cardinals lost often to the Dodgers, mostly without incident, and finished the season in second place, five games behind Brooklyn.

While all this was going on, I was neither a crusader nor a social commentator. I was a baseball announcer. And as a baseball announcer, I knew one thing. Jackie Robinson was—and remains to this day, with the possible exception of Willie Mays —the most exciting ballplayer I have ever seen.

Although Jackie played shortstop with the Kansas City Monarchs in the Negro Baseball League, the Dodgers decided he should replace Eddie Stanky at second base. So when they sent him to Montreal to play for their minor-league team there, Jackie had to learn how to play second. But when he first came up to the major leagues, Stanky was still going strong. Jackie had to move to first base.

Now get this: Not only was Jackie Robinson under the most intense personal pressure of any player in the history of baseball, he was playing a position he'd never played before. Think of all the times you read stories today about this player or that player not being able to adjust to a new position, how switching positions affects his hitting or his concentration. Now think of what Jackie Robinson went through. It boggles the mind!

Not to mention that playing first base meant that everyone had a clear shot at him. He was really vulnerable to the bigots —and there were an awful lot of them.

Robinson, at first base, would have his back to the base runners after they hit ground balls. So here would be the runner, charging down the baseline, screaming, "I'm gonna get you, you black _____! I'm gonna hurt you! I'm gonna spike you!"

And Jackie would have to keep his back turned, keep his foot on the bag, and concentrate on making the catch after the throw from one of the other infielders.

Robinson took all that and never said a word, never fought back—at Branch Rickey's insistence. But he took it only for two years. At that point, he decided that he *could* fight back. I guess he'd decided that he'd proved himself as a man and as a ballplayer. So he dropped his passive role and went out of his way to become aggressive, almost belligerent. He'd give the umpires the choke sign, he'd slide into second with his spikes high, he'd make the hard tag.

Robinson was as much as saying to the white ballplayers, "Okay, you bastards. I took it for two years, now let's see if *you* can take it." And they did. Even the most bigoted players had to admire his skills, had to admit that he belonged in the major leagues. By that time, they also realized they *had* to accept it. There was no way they were going to run this guy out of the league.

For five seasons—after his rookie season at first base—Jackie moved to second base. Then left field. And finally third base. And always he played with consummate skill, with All-Star instinct, with pennant-winning ability. He batted .300, he hit more than his share of home runs, and he was unquestionably the greatest base runner who ever lived. Greater than Lou Brock. Greater than Maury Wills. Greater even, I suppose, than Ty Cobb. No one put fear in the hearts of opposing pitchers and catchers once he reached base the way Jackie Robinson did. To watch him dance off first was to watch a great artist at work. To see him go from first to third on a single to left was to see a great painting in progress. To be there when he stole home, as he did with more style and success than anyone else, was to see the finished work of art hanging in the Louvre. No one, absolutely no one, made the game of baseball as exciting as Jackie Robinson did. And no one—especially during those first couple of seasons—did it under more stressful and difficult circumstances.

That's what I saw during those first couple of seasons Jackie Robinson played in the National League, and that's what I talked about over the airwaves. I talked about how he played the game. Just the same way I talked about how Stan Musial and Ralph Kiner and Pee Wee Reese and Andy Pafko and the other great stars of the National League played the game.

Jackie also did one other thing I had a keen appreciation for —he sold tickets. The seats in the right-field pavilion of Sportsman's Park had rarely been occupied to their capacity before Robinson started playing. But after he broke the barrier, there was never an empty seat when the Dodgers were in town.

So it went, too, in places where the seating wasn't segregated —in Boston and Chicago and Pittsburgh. When the Dodgers would go barnstorming, playing teams from Florida up throughout the South, you could barely get in to see them. And people weren't turning out just to see a baseball game. They were there to see Jackie Robinson. I think one of the things to be considered when deciding what to pay a player is his ability to draw fans. *Nobody* could draw like Jackie. I bet he paid for his whole year's salary in one week of barnstorming. As Wendell Smith, the late black sportswriter who was instrumental in helping Robinson through that 1947 season, wrote with pride:

> *Jackie's nimble,*
> *Jackie's quick,*
> *Jackie's making the turnstiles click.*

Robinson attracted a new and important audience to major-league baseball—America's blacks. Not only did they come to watch him play, but I knew they were also listening to the broadcasts. And I treated them with the same respect and fairness I've always tried to treat anyone else with. It was right, it was reasonable, and, to be honest, it was just good business. Black listeners could buy Griesedieck Brothers beer just the same as white listeners.

I learned, however, that just being fair does not make you immune to criticism. Believe me, I got a lot of criticism about the way I talked about Jackie Robinson. You should see the mail I got. If I complimented Jackie for making a brilliant play, for being a great ballplayer, I'd get a letter—without a return address and written in some barely decipherable chicken scrawl— that started out, "Dear Nigger Lover." But since I had made the decision to treat Jackie Robinson just the way I treated every other ballplayer, I also criticized him. If he made a mistake, I told my listeners about it. If he made a bad play, I said so. And that got his supporters angry. It was a no-win situation. I got angry letters from whites *and* blacks. But I never really paid attention to those letters. I figured they meant that I was doing the job I wanted to do.

Generally, I was popular with black listeners. I think they understood that I was honest, and they appreciated that. In time, the brewery came to realize it could capitalize on my popularity in St. Louis's black neighborhoods. Griesedieck Brothers was the second-biggest-selling beer in the area then, and the reason it wasn't number one was that it did very poorly in the city's black areas. So one day they called me in with an offer they said I could refuse.

They told me of the problems they were having with sales in the black neighborhoods, and asked me if I would mind visiting taverns in those neighborhoods with brewery salesmen to try to drum up interest in the beer.

The way they explained it, they would give me cash and I would go into the taverns, buy drinks for the house, drink Griesedieck, and talk sports with the customers.

There was no way I was going to refuse. I loved the idea. I was tickled to death. They were going to pay my expenses and give me a few bucks on the side to do what I would have been doing anyway—talking sports with people I enjoy. How could I pass it up?

Three things happened during these escapades:

We boosted the hell out of Griesedieck sales in the black neighborhoods.

I made a lot of friends.

And I learned about the broom trick, which, as a communicator, enthralled me.

The broom trick was a simple and effective means of communicating. It worked like this:

I would walk into a saloon and order a round for the house. Now one of the things I realized right away was that even though I was there to push Griesedieck Brothers, I couldn't just go in and order Griesedieck beer for everybody. If you're there to make friends, you've got to give people what they want. Try to force something down their throats and they'll resent it. I was there to promote goodwill as well as the brewery, so that's what I did. Now when I started ordering, there'd be maybe five or six customers in the place. One of those customers would excuse himself and head for the men's room in the back. But instead of using the john, he would grab a broom, go out the back door, and wave the broom around. That meant there was a live one in the joint. Next thing you knew, half the neighborhood would be in there—those five or six customers would magically become twenty-five or fifty—and we would all be having one hell of a party on Griesedieck Brothers.

It was a great way to make friends. And a couple of decades later, it turned out to be a fortuitous development, for which I would be very, very grateful.

In 1971, I was working in Chicago for the White Sox, but I was in St. Louis to do a talk show. When the show was over, I met friends for a drink at the Chase-Park Plaza Hotel. We had more than one. And by the time we left the hotel, it was extremely late—or early, depending on your point of view.

My friends and I said our good-byes and went our separate ways. Their way was to a nearby garage. My way was to my car, which was parked out on Maryland Avenue. My car wouldn't start. I went back to the hotel and called the auto club. They told me to go back and wait in the car for the repair truck to show up.

I followed their instructions. And after I had been waiting a few minutes, I saw two bright headlights come up behind me. I figured it was the auto club, so I jumped out of my car.

It was two black guys. They were clearly not with the auto club. They were each better than 6'6", they both wore beanie caps and ascots, and they both were holding pistols that appeared to be a yard long.

I immediately put my hands up. Just the way they do in the movies. And I started talking.

"Hey, hey, fellas," I said. "Come on. Don't do anything you're going to be sorry for."

One of them told me to be quiet, but then the other looked at me with a funny expression and moved a little closer.

"Hey," he said. "Aren't you Harry Caray?" And with that, he dropped his gun to his side.

When I said that, sure, I *was* Harry Caray, the other guy started jumping up and down, which meant that his gun was waving back and forth right in front of my face.

"Holy cow! Holy cow!" he said. "It *is* Harry Caray! It *is* Harry Caray!"

"Hey, Harry," the first one said, "what are you doing now?"

"You dummy," the second one said, "he's in Chicago. Ain't that right, Harry?"

I couldn't believe what was happening. But I wasn't going to stop playing along now.

"Yeah, yeah, I'm in Chicago," I enthused.

"You got Richie Allen up there, don't you?" the second one asked. "Tell me about Richie Allen, man."

Now I forgot I was being held up. They forgot they were holding me up. And we wound up talking baseball for fifteen minutes.

Finally, one of them said, "Hey, Harry, what the hell are you doing out here this late?"

The other one said—and I really had to laugh, even then—"Yeah, you haven't become one of *us*, have you?"

I told them that wasn't the case, and I explained about how my car wouldn't start.

"No problem," they told me. "Get in the car. We'll get it started."

"Thanks," I said. "But I've called the auto club. They'll be here any minute."

They looked at each other, realized they'd better vamoose, shook my hand, patted me on the back, told me they really missed me, and got right the hell out of there.

Now, up until then, I'd been just as casual and normal and natural as I could be with them. But the minute their car was out of sight, I got this delayed reaction. My body started to shake. Sweat started to pour out of me.

Almost immediately after that, the auto club showed up. The repairman jumped out of his truck with a big smile on his face.

"Harry, as soon as we found out it was you, we gave you special priority," he said. "We would have been here sooner, except we were real busy and . . ."

Then he just stopped. He noticed that I was sweating profusely and shaking like a leaf.

"What's the matter, Harry?" he wanted to know. "You feel all right?"

"Yeah, yeah, I'm fine."

"You sure?" he pressed. "You don't look too good. Anything I can do to help?"

"Just get the car started," I said. "If I told you the story, you'd never believe me."

And as he went to work on my car, one thing came to mind. A memory from long before.

When I used to go to Sportsman's Park, I'd drive my Oldsmobile convertible through the black area on Spring Avenue. I'd always wave to the kids playing on the sidewalk and to their folks sitting out on their porches. They'd all wave and yell back. Whenever someone was in the car with me, I'd always say, "I'm telling you, these are my people. These are my people." And the first thing I thought of, after that incident in 1971, was that they *were* my people.

And was I glad.

Jackie Robinson had one other rather unusual effect on my life. He unwittingly helped me get a raise.

It was about a year after Robinson had broken the barrier, sometime during the middle of the 1948 season. I was negotiating a new contract with Oscar Zahner and the brewery. For a change, I was dealing from strength. I was not an unknown anymore. So Oscar decided that the way to do business with me was to sweet-talk me, to wine and dine me. That's what he was doing this particular evening.

But I was having none of it. Oscar had taken me to dinner and a show, but I still wouldn't budge. I had read in the newspapers that Dizzy Dean, who was doing the Browns' games for Falstaff with Buddy Blattner, was making twenty-five thousand dollars a season. I was making about half that much, which I didn't think was too fair. I wanted to make what Dizzy was making.

When we came out of the theater, we were still arguing about it. Oscar was making the same points he'd already made over and over during the evening. Dizzy was a big national name. He was such a big personality in town that he commanded a lot of newspaper attention. Dizzy Dean made headlines, Oscar said. Harry Caray didn't.

Just then—it was in front of the Orpheum Theater, if I remember correctly—we heard a newsboy hawking the bulldog edition, the early edition of the next morning's *Globe-Democrat*.

"Read all about it! Read all about it!" he was crying. "Harry Caray's life threatened!"

I looked at Oscar. He looked at me. And neither of us knew what the hell was going on.

I ran over to the corner, pushed my way through the gathering crowd, gave the newsboy a buck, and took two newspapers. Sure enough, there it was: a big, bold headline that said HARRY CARAY GETS DEATH THREAT. And right smack dab in the middle of the front page was a picture of me. I ran back to Oscar and shoved one of the papers in front of him.

"Take a look at this," I crowed. "Tell me something. Did Dizzy Dean ever get a headline like that?"

We both laughed. We both knew I was going to get my raise

now. Then we stopped laughing, at least I did. I had to make sure I was going to live long enough to get this raise.

I read the newspaper to find out who wanted to kill me.

It turned out that some lunatic racist had written a letter to Fred Saigh, who had not long before bought the Cardinals from Sam Breadon. The letter writer threatened to kill Harry Caray *and* the Cardinals, and bomb their ballpark, if Jackie Robinson was allowed to play in St. Louis again.

Ordinarily, this was the kind of letter you would just throw in the trash can. But Fred Saigh was an attorney who had had experience with things like this. Earlier in his career, Saigh had been the attorney for Spyros Skouras, the old movie mogul. Skouras had once received a similar letter and ignored it. And he almost paid the price, because a few days after tossing the letter away, the writer jumped on the running board of Skouras's limousine and tried to shoot him. Fortunately, he missed, but Saigh never forgot the incident. So, without telling me, he turned this new letter over to the FBI.

Well, the next day at the ballpark, the Dodgers opened a series against the Cardinals. The stands were packed, as they always were for the Dodgers. I was strolling around, saying hello to Jackie Robinson, Duke Snider, Pee Wee Reese, Roy Campanella, Carl Furillo, and others, when I had this eerie feeling that somebody was following me. Sure enough, *two* somebodies were following me. Two big guys right on my tail.

"What do you guys think you're doing?" I asked.

"FBI, Harry," they explained, and showed me their identification. "We're going to follow you around for a while, until we're sure you're in no danger."

And those guys were good, too. No matter what I did, I couldn't shake them. And it got a little embarrassing, I'll tell you. There were a few places I wanted to go and a few things I wanted to do, but I couldn't, because these guys were always on top of me. After a few days, it cooled off, though. They were convinced that no one was going to kill me, so they went back to crime-busting. Much to my relief, I was able to go back to having fun.

The strange thing was, in all my years in St. Louis, I rarely got my name in the newspapers unless something negative occurred: if there was a death threat or if I got divorced—as happened several times—or if I got fired.

I'll never forget the time of my first divorce.

Adlai Stevenson, the governor of Illinois, our neighboring state, got sued for divorce. The same day.

The story about Governor Stevenson—who would *twice* be the Democratic nominee for president—ran on page thirty-three of the *Globe-Democrat.*

The story of my divorce ran on page one.

A banner headline.

There was a big picture of me, wearing a T-shirt, in action in the booth. Below the photo, in big block letters, the caption said, HOLY COW, HE'S OUT! Then, in slightly smaller letters just below that, in parentheses, it said, "(At Home)."

Several weeks later, I ran into the publisher of the paper. And I confronted him. I felt perfectly justified. No matter whose fault a divorce is—and in this case, most of the fault was mine—it's a traumatic experience. I didn't like seeing it turned into a tabloid story.

"Why in the world did you have to plaster my divorce all over the front page?" I wanted to know. "There was nothing there. It didn't warrant that kind of treatment."

He had a ready alibi. "Harry," he said, "my business is selling newspapers."

I understood that and told him so. "But Governor Stevenson got sued for divorce the same day, and that story was buried way the hell in the back of the paper!"

Now he smiled.

"You ought to feel proud. Governor Stevenson doesn't sell newspapers. You do."

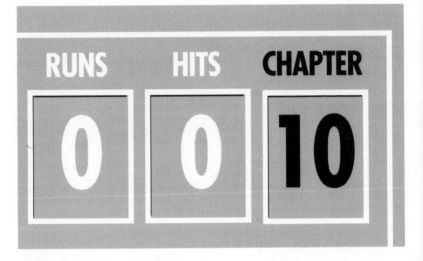

RUNS   HITS   CHAPTER

0   0   10

Earlier, I mentioned that Jackie Robinson and Willie Mays were the most exciting baseball players I've ever seen. And that's true. But that doesn't mean they were the best.

When I am asked to name the best player I've ever seen, I don't have to think about it. It's not even a debatable question as far as I'm concerned. The answer is simple.

Stan Musial.

Stan Musial did more things for the game—on the field and off—than anyone else who ever played.

Sure, a case could be made that Ted Williams was the greatest pure hitter who ever lived. Those who saw him day in and day out say Joe DiMaggio was the most complete ballplayer of his time. Willie Mays was probably the most complete of his generation. Henry Aaron, surprisingly, was the greatest power hitter. No one realized that Hammerin' Hank was quietly hitting thirty-nine, forty, forty-one home runs every year. For a lot of years.

Nobody—and I mean *nobody*—had more natural talent than Mickey Mantle. If he'd not been injured, I think Mantle would have rewritten all the records. No one played with more grace and élan than Roberto Clemente.

I know all the arguments, and I can't refute any of them.

Still, if I were starting a club from scratch and all the players I have ever seen were available to me, Stan Musial would be my first draft choice.

Musial was not really a big man. He was 6' tall and, during his younger days, about 175 pounds. He hit with power. And as Gabby Street used to point out, hitters like Ted Williams were so disciplined that they'd take a pitch an inch or two off the plate and draw a base on balls. But Musial would swing at those pitches —if he thought it was more important to the team for him to get a hit. Stan felt responsible for his team. He wanted to win.

Musial was durable. He rarely missed a game because of injury or illness. He broke in with the Cardinals at the end of the 1941 season. He played until 1963, and until that final season there was no measurable drop-off in his performance, besides his speed. In fact, in 1962, when he was forty-one years old, he played in 135 games, hit 19 home runs, knocked in 82 runs, and batted .330. If he had that kind of season in 1986, he would be looking for a $10-million, five-year, no-cut contract. Before the 1962 season, no less an expert than Branch Rickey wrote that Stan was washed up and should retire.

Stan Musial had the statistics. He had 3,630 hits, the National League record until Pete Rose came along. He hit 475 home runs. His evolution as a home-run hitter took some time. He had a lightning-fast swing, and his reputation was made as someone who hit wicked line drives into right center and left center. But he learned how to hit the long ball. Look at his 177 triples and 725 doubles. That's 1,377 extra base hits.

Only Hank Aaron—with 1,477—has more. Stan had 6,134 total bases. A lifetime slugging percentage of .559. He scored 1,949 runs, knocked in 1,951. He is eighth on the all-time list of most walks, with 1,599. Yet he only struck out 696 times— many, many fewer than any of the 15 other players in baseball history who hit as many as 475 home runs in their careers. And, of course, there is the stuff everyone remembers. He won the Most Valuable Player Award three times, the National League batting title seven times, and had a career batting average of .331, the highest of any player whose career ended as recently as 1963.

Stan Musial was a winner. He played in four World Series for the Cardinals and they won three. He played twenty-two seasons, and only five times (in the six seasons between 1954 and 1959) did the Cardinals lose more games than they won.

But the statistics and the won-lost record do not *begin* to tell the story of Stan Musial; they do not begin to explain why he is my all-time baseball hero, or why on the Harry Caray All-Stars or in the Harry Caray Hall of Fame he would be the first person selected. With Stan Musial, it runs deeper than facts you can discover in the box scores or the standings or the record books. Much deeper.

But before we go any further, we ought to get one thing straight. I don't have this great, unwavering admiration for Stan Musial because he was or is one of my pals. Sure, I probably saw Stan play more than anyone else saw him play. And, yes, I spent a great deal of time around him at the ballpark and on the road during our seasons together. But while Stan and I are friends, we were never buddies, running mates. We didn't go in the same crowd—which was a good thing for him. It probably added years to his career.

If I were to name my all-time team, Stan would be my captain.

He was a great leader, a great team man. Moreover, Stan never forgot what baseball did for him when he was playing, and he still hasn't forgotten. For almost five decades, Stan has given back more than he took. Baseball afforded Musial fame and fortune, but no man has worn success better.

I remember many of Stan's great plays, many of his big hits and spectacular days. In particular, I remember Sunday, May 2, 1954, which might have been his best day of all. The Cardinals were playing the New York Giants in a double header, and I called every inning.

In the first inning of the first game, Musial lined one of left-hander Johnny Antonelli's infrequent hanging curveballs into the right-field pavilion for a home run.

In the fifth inning, with Red Schoendienst on base, Musial hit a fly ball to right off an Antonelli fastball. Years later, someone told me my call sounded something like this:

"Long fly ball to right. Way back. It might be out of here. It IS! A home run for Stan 'the Man' Musial. Holy cow! His second of the day."

I don't know what happened to the "It could be . . ." but that still sounds about right.

A couple of innings later, Jim Hearn, working in relief of Antonelli, failed to get a slider past Musial. The poor guy never had a chance. I have been told I got the whole call out that time, the whole "it might be, it could be, it IS!" sequence. Which, of course, was exactly what the occasion deserved. Stan had never before hit three home runs in a game.

In the nightcap, Hoyt Wilhelm, the great knuckleballer who was inducted into the Hall of Fame in 1985, was working for the Giants. Stan never had much luck against knuckleball pitchers. As he used to say, "By the time the ball gets to the plate, it's somewhere else from where you last saw it." Wilhelm probably should have kept that in mind. But he didn't. The first time he faced Stan in that second game, he tried to sneak a curveball by him. It didn't work. Stan hit another home run, his fourth, to right field.

The next time Stan hit, Wilhelm was still pitching. This at bat, Musial said later, was one of the few times in his career when he went to the plate thinking "home run." And, of course, he got it, even though Wilhelm—not repeating the mistakes of the recent past—threw nothing but knucklers.

No one ever had hit five home runs in one day. And as I recall, Musial hit three more balls right on the nose, each time sending Willie Mays toward the flagpole in center field. Those shots could have gone out, too. Musial could have hit eight home runs in one day. It is probably the greatest exhibition of hitting in one day ever in the major leagues.

Of course, there's a lot more to Stan Musial than home runs and record-breaking feats. I remember him most for the personal side, the things he used to do away from the ballpark. The things he used to do for the people who helped make him what he was—the fans.

It can get awfully hot in St. Louis, sometimes reaching 110 degrees on the field during a hot summer afternoon. But even after a long double header—whether he went 0-for-8 or hit 5 home runs—Stan was forever Stan the Man. It would be six-thirty, maybe seven o'clock in the evening. The end of a long day, a day of eighteen innings, unbearable heat, and matching humidity. The kind of day that drains most men, that irritates them, that leaves them kicking the dog. But it never seemed to affect the temperament or personality of Stan Musial.

Just outside the ballpark, in the players' parking lot, there would always be a group of kids—a hundred of them, maybe two hundred—waiting for autographs. At the end of one of those marathon dog-day doubleheaders, other ballplayers might duck the crowd. And who could blame them, really?

But when Musial came out, it was different. When the kids saw him coming, they would all gather around his car (his Cadillac was always parked in the same spot, just across from the press entrance to the ballpark). They would part and let him reach the door to the car. Once he was there, he would turn around, lean against the car, and stand there and sign autographs for as long as it took to satisfy everyone. Forty-five minutes, an hour, it didn't matter. Stan would not flinch. He would not complain. He would always have a smile or a kind word. He even carried pictures of himself to give away. He figured it was just as much a part of his job as hitting home runs or making great catches. And he was right, of course. I think it's a real shame that more athletes haven't developed Musial's sense of and flair for public relations.

I guess, in all these years, Stan has never forgotten his roots. He has never forgotten how lucky he has been. He has never forgotten that, were it not for baseball, he might still be working in the mills or mines of his hometown of Donora, Pennsylvania —working, that is, if he had not already died in an industrial accident or from black lung.

Stan never forgot, either, how close he was to washing out as a ballplayer. When the Cardinals first signed him, he was a pitcher, and, as it turned out, not a very good one. For three years, he was stuck in Class D ball, making maybe sixty-five bucks a month. He just wasn't good enough for the Cards to move him up the ladder. Then, one day when he was horsing around in the outfield, he dived for a sinking line drive and injured his pitching shoulder.

Trying to get their money's worth out of Musial, the Class D club decided to use him as an occasional outfielder until his pitching shoulder healed. All of a sudden, it seemed that every time he played, he got three or four hits. This came to the attention of Branch Rickey. And it didn't take Rickey long to figure out that Musial's future looked a lot brighter as a left-handed hitting outfielder than it did as a perpetual Class D pitcher.

Within several months, Musial went from Class D to Class B to Class A, to Double A, to Triple A, and he actually finished the last two weeks of that season in the big leagues with the St. Louis Cardinals.

He never looked back.

One last thing about Rickey. Not only did he have the foresight to promote Musial quickly through the farm system, he was smart enough not to tamper with Stan's unorthodox swing.

When Stan was at the plate, he had this odd crouch. He kind of peeked around the corner at the ball as it came in from the pitcher, and he swung with a corkscrew motion. Rickey was perceptive enough to forbid anyone to change Musial's swing. He didn't even want anyone to *talk* to Stan about his swing.

Today, I'm sure most managers and coaches would try to make a guy with that swing conform to the norm. But Branch Rickey saw that Stan Musial could hit, even if he didn't look pretty. And Rickey's theory was, "If it isn't broken, don't try to fix it."

There aren't a lot of guys like Musial around anymore. There aren't a lot of guys like Williams around, or DiMaggio or Mays or Aaron or Mantle or Robinson, either. But there is a fellow right now who reminds me very much of Stan Musial. It's George Brett. He does everything you would want a ballplayer to do and more. He sure hits like Musial—to right center, left center, down the line. George may not be as fast as Stan was in his prime. But if there's anyone who can be compared to my baseball idol, it's George Brett—on the field and off.

Now all of those fellows I just mentioned would certainly be on the Harry Caray All-Stars. But there are a few more spots on the roster, and I want to fill them. I'm only going to select guys I've seen often enough to really judge.

My catchers would be Johnny Bench—he's probably the greatest who ever lived—and Roy Campanella. Walker Cooper was great, too. For my pitching staff, I would want Bob Gibson, the best right-hander I ever saw, and Sandy Koufax, the best left-hander I ever saw. With those two, I know we're going to win half our games regardless of who makes up the rest of the staff.

I would put Musial at first, although that's really cheating, because most of his career was spent in the outfield.

Jackie Robinson would be at second. But there have been a lot of good ones at that position. Rod Carew was great. Red Schoendienst, too, was an outstanding second baseman. And the young man on the Cubs now has a chance to be the best of them all before he's through. I'm referring to Ryne Sandberg.

At shortstop, it's got to be Marty Marion, though it's almost impossible to pick between Luis Aparicio, Pee Wee Reese, and Phil Rizzuto among the veterans, and Cal Ripken and Ozzie Guillen today. And how can you leave off a guy who hit 512 home runs? Maybe we could employ a platoon system. Ernie Banks will hit as our shortstop, and Marty Marion and Pee Wee Reese will field.

I know a lot of people think Ozzie Smith of the Cardinals is one of the greatest fielders of all time. But he's an astroturf player. Fielding on astroturf is an entirely different skill. He's the best there is on synthetic turf—he's rewritten the book—but

I don't think Ozzie Smith stacks up to the great grass fielders.

At third base, I've got George Brett. But how do I leave off Brooks Robinson? Or Mike Schmidt or Kenny Boyer or Graig Nettles? That's why I don't like making up All-Star teams. There are too many great players.

It's practically impossible to select the three best outfielders. You'd have to start with Babe Ruth. But you'd also have to find a way to work Mays, Aaron, DiMaggio, Mantle, Clemente, Williams, Snider, Kaline, and Frank Robinson into the lineup.

And that lineup card will be brought out, of course, by our captain, Stan Musial, the greatest baseball player I have ever seen.

RUNS   HITS   CHAPTER

0   0   11

I've always looked forward to the next place I go. And when I'm there, I don't want to miss anything.

I've been traveling on the road for forty-one years. I found it enthralling when I started, I find it just as exciting now. I get a charge out of it. Renewing old friendships in each town I pass through. Eating and drinking in old, familiar places. Discovering new ones. People, when they discuss my job, always mention the boredom of traveling. I've never understood that. I think life on the road is anything *but* boring.

Cities, like ballplayers, have their own character. And I like to find it. When a ball game is over and my workday finished, I like to stop in the press room for a drink, bid my good-byes, leave the ballpark, and do the town. If someone wants to come along, fine. If not, I'll go it alone.

Even before I moved there, Chicago was my favorite town. When the Cards or the A's would play there, I always opened

my broadcast by singing "My kind of town, Chicago is"—
though not quite as well as Frank Sinatra does it.

When I was in the American League, I got to go to Boston
several times a year. That town is always a delight.

My taste doesn't run only to American cities. Here's a good
bit of trivia. Did you know that I was the first broadcaster to do
a major-league game in Montreal *and* Toronto? That's right.
The first game the Expos ever played in Montreal was against
the Cardinals—so I did the first National League game in Can-
ada. And several years later, when I was working for the White
Sox, it was the Sox who were the Blue Jays' opponent when they
opened in Toronto—the first American League game to be
played north of the American border.

Montreal's a good place to play, but it was a tough place to
play baseball before they put a roof on Olympic Stadium.

I remember going up to Montreal with the Cardinals that first
time. It was right after spring training. When we pulled in from
Florida, on a Sunday, there were about six inches of snow. The
same thing on Monday. So everybody assumed there'd be no
game. We just went out, had a good time, and didn't worry
about the next day. But lo and behold, I woke up at seven-thirty
Tuesday morning, and it's seventy degrees outside. The sun was
shining; the game was clearly going to be played.

The grounds keepers managed to get the snow off the field,
but the ground was completely frozen. However, as the game
progressed and the field thawed out, I noticed that the catchers
had sunk down to their ankles. They were practically embedded
in the mud.

Toronto surprised me as a city. I don't exactly know what I
was expecting, but I like it a lot. The same thing with Seattle.
I used to love it when the White Sox went out to play the
Mariners. It's a beautiful city.

New York, of course, was the first place on the road that really captured my imagination. I wanted to meet and get to know the city I'd been reading about for all those years in Walter Winchell's and Jimmy Cannon's columns. It was a new world for me, but it was a world I took to naturally. I was never intimidated by Manhattan, or its size or reputation. I seemed to fit right in.

I'm not much for museums or art galleries, to be honest. I'm more of the saloon type. But one of the first things I did when I got to New York City was go to the Statue of Liberty. I have to admit, that did get to me. I also have to admit that the reason I went there was because I was with my young son, Skip.

The first place I learned about when I went to New York were the after-hours clubs. There was one called the Golden Key Club, and that joint was always hopping. I was in there the night that Billy Daniels got cut up by a jealous girlfriend.

Then, after a while, I started to live at the Copacabana. The Copa was the classiest nightclub of them all. The greatest entertainers in the country used to perform there. You walked down those few steps below the elegant curved awning on Sixtieth Street between Madison and Fifth, and it was like leaving the world behind. It was like walking into a movie. The place was always loaded with celebrities. There would be your movie star here, your shipping mogul there, your financier here, and always a few uptown gangsters sprinkled in for color and style. You could see anybody and anything in that joint.

I used to go in the Copa lounge early in the evening to have a drink before going out to dinner. It got to be sort of a habit. And almost every time I went in there, I would see the same fellow—impeccably dressed—sitting all alone in the back booth, very gentlemanly nursing a drink. After a while, we started to nod to each other, then wave. Then one day I told the bartender to send him over a drink. A little later, he sent a drink back to me. And exchanging drinks became a habit, too. But that was it. Never a conversation. Never a hello. Never even a thank you. There was sort of a gentlemen's code of the saloon at work here, and neither of us was inclined to break it.

This went on for one whole season. Whenever I was in New York, I'd go to the Copa, and whenever I was in the Copa, I'd be exchanging drinks with this guy I didn't know.

The next year, we came into New York for our first series of the season, and sure enough, when I hit the Copa, the same guy's sitting there in his usual booth.

I leaned over to the bartender and finally asked, "Who is that guy?"

The bartender looked at me as if I were crazy.

"Harry, you're not kidding me, are you?" he asked.

"No," I told him.

"You *really* don't know who that is?"

"No," I insisted. "Who is he?"

"Harry," he said, "that's Frank Costello."

Frank Costello was one of those uptown gangster types I mentioned before. Except bigger. His business associates and running mates were fellows with names like Lucky Luciano and Bugsy Siegel and Meyer Lansky.

I figured we ought to meet.

So I went over to his booth and extended my right hand.

"Gee, Mr. Costello," I said, "I am embarrassed. All this time we've been exchanging drinks, and I really didn't know who you were until just now."

He took my hand warmly and a grin split his face.

"You see, Harry, that's the difference between us," he explained. "From the time you sent over that first drink, I made it a point of knowing who you were."

Then he invited me to sit with him, and we talked sports for a while. He was engaging and he was knowledgeable. It's funny. Over the years, I've met a lot of people in the same line of work as Frank Costello, and they have always seemed to like me. Which is good. I'd much rather have them like me than dislike me. And they've all seemed to be regular people. I have a policy with them. I don't know their business; all I know is what I read in the newspaper. But if a guy sends me a drink, I'm going to return it. I always return the favor. And if a guy wants to sit and talk sports, I will sit and talk sports with him.

Toots Shor was another New York character. He ran one of the best and most famous saloons in the world. A lot of sports people used to hang out in his place.

I remember one time, I got furious at Toots.

I had walked in, as I frequently did when I was in town, and I went up to stand at the bar, which was packed two and three deep. Well, while I was standing there, this little old couple comes in. They couldn't even get to the bar; it was too crowded. I heard them ask one of the bartenders if Mr. Shor was in. The bartender told them that yes, he was in, but he was very busy at the back of the restaurant.

I looked into the dining room and saw that Toots was sitting in one of the booths with, as I recall, Jack Kennedy.

This little old man now said to the bartender, "You know, we came all the way from Dubuque, Iowa. This is our first trip to New York. And we have read so much about Toots Shor, we just wanted to come in here and say hello to him."

Just then Toots came into the bar to bark an order at the bartender. The bartender said to Toots, "Mr. Shor, there's a couple here from Iowa. They came in just because they've read so much about you. I wonder if you could come over and say hello."

Toots Shor looked at his bartender and said, "Who has time for them?" And then he strode back to the dining room.

I heard this and I looked at the little old couple—they were crushed. I felt so, so embarrassed. I went over to them and made a point of starting a conversation with them.

"Hey," I said, "don't pay any attention to that. Toots'll probably be out here pretty soon to say hello." Then I bought them a drink.

Well, Toots never did come back, and the couple finally left.

The next night, I came back to Toots Shor's. He didn't have any of his important friends around, so I went up to Toots and told him what had happened the night before. I laid it on the line and told him I thought it was one of the most terrible things I'd ever heard.

"They paid you the supreme tribute," I ranted. "And what did you do? You wouldn't even go over to say hello!"

Toots was shocked. "Harry, did I do that?"

"Yeah!"

"I didn't go over?"

"No!"

"God, I must have been drunk," he said.

He truly felt bad. But I've never forgotten that. I haven't forgotten it in my personal life or in my business life. It's one of the reasons why, if someone comes up to me and wants to talk or just wants an autograph, I always try to be as nice as I possibly can. What does it cost me? Nothing. And it makes everybody —including me—feel good.

Another place on the circuit where a young fellow could meet some interesting characters was Cincinnati. Well, not exactly Cincinnati, but just across the Ohio River in Covington, Kentucky, which was one hell of a wide-open town. If something was illegal everywhere else, they did it in Covington.

One of those somethings was gambling.

One night, after a ball game, a few of the Cardinal players and I went across the river to a club called the Glen Rendezvous to listen to a young, good-looking singer one of the players happened to know. When her show was over, the singer invited us to follow her upstairs, to the gambling club.

Before we got very far into the room, I got entranced by a dice game. It wasn't craps. It was something I think they called Keno, though it was nothing like the Keno they play in Las Vegas today. Anyway, I was entranced by this shill who put on a terrific show every time he rolled the dice. So I stopped and watched him and got the hang of the game. I'm not much of a gambler —except for a good game of gin—but if I remember correctly, in this game the object was to reach a certain number of points. It seemed simple enough.

After my first roll, it seemed even simpler. Whatever it took to win, I was only two points away. I rolled again. Didn't make it. So I rolled again. Didn't make it. And again. And again. Then one of the other players dropped out and I took over *his* bet— so I was now playing for twice as much money. Several of the players told me to quit, but I refused. How hard could it be to make a measly two points? I'll tell you how hard. Many rolls and $5,480 later, I still had not made those points.

By now, it was almost sunrise. As determined as I was to win, I finally had to concede. I was practically the only person in the casino. It was time to get out of there.

Naturally, I didn't have enough cash to meet my obligation, so I wrote out a personal check to cover my losses and presented it to the casino.

Benny Stevens, a nice little fellow who owned a jazz joint in

Cincinnati, then offered me a ride back to my hotel, the grand old Netherlands Hilton, which has just recently been restored to its former glory.

During the trip across the river, we reviewed what had happened to me at the dice table. Benny listened carefully.

"You know, you can't ever say I told this to you," he said. "But, Harry, you got to stop payment on that check."

"Oh, I can't do that," I responded. "I can't welsh on a thing like that. Gambling's legal over there. Besides, I don't want to be known as a welsher."

"Yeah," Benny said, "but you didn't have a chance."

"What do you mean I didn't have a chance?"

"There was no way you could've made that extra two points."

"You sure?" I asked.

"Please, Harry, don't ask me any more questions, but yes, I'm sure." Those were Benny's final words on the subject.

By the time I got up to my room on the twelfth floor of the hotel, I was seriously beginning to consider Benny's advice. I wasn't sure I would stop payment, but I was at least going to think about it.

Just as I opened the door, the phone rang. This was at about six-thirty in the morning. I wasn't used to getting calls at that hour. I picked up the phone.

"Harry Caray? You had a tough night at the Glen Rendezvous," a voice said.

"Yeah," I responded. "Who is this?"

"Stop payment on the check," the man said. And then he hung up the phone.

Now I was really in a quandry. This was the second time in fifteen minutes I had received the same advice. I waited about an hour, because of the time difference, and then I called my lawyer in St. Louis, Jack Giesecke.

I related the whole story.

"Well, let's stop payment on the check," he advised.

"Jack, I don't want to be labeled as a welsher."

"You don't have to welsh. Just stop payment. See what happens, and if you have to pay, you just restore the check. That's no problem."

"All right," I said. "I hope you know what you're talking about."

So I called the bank and stopped payment on my check.

And for twenty-four hours, nothing happened. But the next afternoon, while I was in my room getting ready to go to the ballpark, the phone rang. Before I could say even hello, the voice, which sounded like it was being filtered by sandpaper, was saying, "My name is Tony Baker."

I brightened. I figured if he was telling me his name, he was a fan looking to talk baseball or maybe get a couple of tickets or have me say hello on the air to someone back in St. Louis.

"Yes, sir," I said.

"You shouldn't have done what you did," he went on.

"What's that?"

"Stopped payment on that check," he replied.

Now I began to get real nervous again.

"I'm in the lobby. I want you to come down here immediately," he ordered. "I'll be at the bar."

"I don't know what you look like," I mentioned rather feebly.

"Don't worry," he said. "I know what *you* look like."

I hung up, and I was shaking like a leaf. I figured, Uh-oh, they're gonna find me in pieces in an alley or something. But I went down there just the way he said I should and met him.

"You shouldn't have done that." He glowered.

I couldn't even respond.

"You know what this could lead to, don't you?"

I weakly acknowledged that I did.

"So why did you do it?"

"Well, I just figured that after all those rolls of the dice, if I couldn't make two lousy points, it must have been impossible."

Now he got very indignant.

"You know," he shouted, "we have one of the most recognized and honest gambling houses in the world. And you know gambling is legal."

"Oh, yes. That's why I was there. Because it's legal," I answered.

"Well, all right," he said. "I have this check here that you stopped payment on. You don't want to call it even and settle for this fifty-five hundred bucks, right?"

Now, as he was saying this, he was indicating to me with his head that I was supposed to answer no. I was supposed to say that I *didn't* want to settle for fifty-five hundred. Confused, I obliged him. I said no.

"And you don't want to settle for forty-five hundred, either, do you?" And again he gave me the indication that my answer should be no.

"And you don't want to settle for four grand," he said. And the same thing happened. Thirty-five hundred. Three thousand. Two thousand.

He worked his way all the way down to five hundred bucks.

"For five hundred dollars, you'd be happy to settle right now, wouldn't you?" And this time he was nodding his head vigorously.

"Oh, yeah, yeah, right, right," I said. "Five hundred dollars."

And I reached into my pocket to get my checkbook. He suddenly stopped nodding.

"Uh-uh," he said. "Cash only."

I asked him to wait just a minute, and I ran up the stairs from the lobby to the office of Harry Nolan, the hotel manager. I wrote out a check for five hundred dollars and gave it to him.

"Harry," I said, "give me five hundred cash. Fast."

Harry, thank God, didn't ask any questions. He just gave me the money, and as fast as I could, I ran back down those stairs and returned to Tony Baker.

I handed him the cash and started to thank him. "This is really nice," I gushed. "I sure do appreciate it."

He cut me off. "Don't you want your check back?" he wanted to know.

This hadn't even occurred to me, I was so flustered. Of course I told him that I did, and he handed me back the check.

I would live to love another day, and I had just saved myself five grand. I was thrilled and relieved. I also figured it would be the last I would ever hear of the incident.

It wasn't.

A few months later, on a Saturday night after broadcasting a St. Louis University basketball game from old Kiel Auditorium, I went out to a place I frequented called the Victorian Club. It was *the* place to be seen in St. Louis at the time, the carriage-trade favorite.

The place was jammed that night. As I stood at the piano bar, I noticed a gentleman named Murph. Murph was known as a gambling czar, and he was a heck of a nice guy. So I sent him a drink. He returned the favor. And a few minutes later, as he apparently was going to the bathroom, he passed within a couple of feet of me.

"How'd the game come out?" he asked.

"The Billikens won," I responded.

"How many points?" he wanted to know.

"Three," I said, with a shrug. I should have known he would've been interested in the point spread rather than the actual outcome of the game.

"That's good," he replied. "By the way, how'd you make out with that Glen Rendezvous thing?"

"Fine, fine," I said. "How'd you know about that?"

He looked at me as if I had just told him two and two were five.

"You half-guinea jerk." He laughed. "Why do you think you got off for only five hundred bucks?"

"What?" I didn't know what he was talking about.

"I own a piece of that place," he said. "They called me about your check. I told them you're a nice guy and I didn't want to see you get hurt, but that I wanted you to pay for the lesson. I told them to accept five hundred from you."

"Well, I'll be damned."

"See, you cast your bread upon the waters," he said, "and sometimes it actually pays a dividend. You're a nice guy, Harry. We like you here. We appreciate the job you do. We don't need your money. But I hope you learned a lesson about Keno."

And let me tell you, I really had. But I still had a couple more lessons to learn about gambling.

In all my life, I had never bet on baseball or on any other sport. But in 1966, I couldn't resist. The Dodgers were going to play the Baltimore Orioles in the World Series. I figured there was no way the star-studded Dodgers could lose, not with Sandy Koufax, Don Drysdale, Maury Wills, Willie Davis, Tommy Davis, and all those other great players. The Orioles were a bunch of youngsters (of course, who could know they'd become such experienced stars as Jim Palmer, Dave McNally, Brooks Robinson, and Mark Belanger?). They just didn't have the prestige—or, I was sure, the ability—of the more famous Dodgers.

I was in Busch's Grove, one of my favorite hangouts, and we were talking about the World Series. The conversation got around to gambling with Claude Turner, the bartender. He and some of the customers were talking about odds, which were always something of a mystery to me. Claude, an affable guy, explained to me that the Dodgers were favored by sixteen to ten. This meant that if you bet sixteen hundred dollars on the Dodgers, you could win a thousand dollars if they took the Series, while if you bet a thousand dollars on the underdog Orioles, you would win sixteen hundred dollars if they won.

Even though it was risking sixteen hundred to win a thousand, I thought the Dodgers were a sure thing. I didn't think it was possible for them to lose. So the more I thought about it, the more I thought, Hey, how can I let this opportunity pass?

"Listen, Claude," I said, "I've never made a bet in my life. But I sure would like to put up that sixteen hundred dollars on the Dodgers."

He told me I had a deal. No problem.

Well, you know what happened in 1966. The Los Angeles Dodgers were beaten by the young Orioles in four straight games. The Dodgers scored two runs in that first game and then were shut out in the next three.

But I still hadn't learned my lesson.

Three years later, the same Orioles—only now they were older, more experienced, and carried the same kind of prestige as the 1966 Dodgers—were in the World Series playing against the upstart New York Mets. This time I was just as sure about the Orioles as I had been about the 1966 Dodgers. So I went back to Busch's Grove, had a conversation with Claude Turner, and made a similar investment. The odds were even the same —Baltimore was favored sixteen to ten.

Once again I bet sixteen hundred dollars on experience and prestige.

And once again, I was consistent. The Mets won four straight games—after losing the first one—and I doubled my career losses on baseball betting.

So this so-called baseball expert has made only two bets in my life, losing sixteen hundred dollars on the first one and another sixteen hundred dollars on the second.

I did actually learn my lesson, just the way I learned it at the Glen Rendezvous.

I lost thirty-two hundred dollars trying to win two thousand. Not only did I learn a gambling lesson, I realized that arithmetic was not one of my strongest subjects.

Perhaps the most unique adventure of my life on the road occurred not during a baseball trip but during college basketball's National Invitational Tournament, which is played annually at New York's Madison Square Garden. I had left spring training in Florida to come up and broadcast a St. Louis University game. This was in the early sixties.

When the game ended, I hustled back to the hotel, showered, shaved, changed, and was ready to do the town. It was the shank of the evening. Right about midnight.

Down in the lobby, I ran into a couple of the sportswriters who were covering the team.

"Come on," I urged. "Why don't you guys come with me? I have a hell of an idea. Let's go up to Harlem."

Now Harlem was a place I'd always wanted to experience. Even though this was long after the era of the Cotton Club, Harlem was still celebrated for its jumping night spots. Count

Basie still had a place where they played music all night long; Wilt Chamberlain owned a joint called Small's Paradise.

I'd read about it, I'd heard about it, but I'd never been there. By now you should have realized something about me—if there's someplace I want to go, eventually I'm going to get there.

The sportswriters in the lobby thought I was crazy. They sarcastically told me to have a swell time but they didn't care to come along. So I set off on my own.

Now I'd tried to go up to Harlem on a few previous occasions. Each time, when I'd gotten in a cab, I'd told the driver where I wanted to go and he'd said, "Sorry, pal. I don't go to Harlem," or words to that effect.

This time I played it smart.

I hailed a taxi, got in, and told the driver to go up to Central Park. When we got to the entrance, I told him I wanted to go through the park. He was a little leery, but he didn't want to blow a pretty decent fare, so he asked, "Sir, where exactly do you want to go?"

There was no point in postponing it. "I want to go to Harlem," I told him. "But I was afraid if I told you that right off the bat, you wouldn't have let me in the cab."

"You're right about that." He grinned.

"You can't kick me out here," I said, " 'cause I've already run up a good fare. So why don't you take me all the way?"

"Well, sir, where do you want to go in Harlem?"

That was a good question. The only problem was that I didn't have an answer. I had no idea where I wanted to go or where I was supposed to go in Harlem. And I told this to the driver.

"You must be nuts," was his response. "Or at least a lot braver than I am."

But he kept driving.

After a while, I said, "Look, you've been driving a hack for a long time. You must have heard about a few of the hot spots, some of the nightclubs up there."

The only place he'd ever heard of was a place called the Baby Grand. He didn't know what it was like, but he did know where it was.

"Good enough," I decided. "Take me there."

I can still see the outside of the Baby Grand vividly. It had a bright marquee, all lit up with bright lights, right in the middle of Harlem, I believe on 125th Street and Lenox Avenue.

I walked through the front door—the only white person in sight. There was this great long bar—the club was in the back —and there must have been six bartenders. I got the attention of one of them, as politely as I could. I was wearing a coat and tie, and I'm pretty sure he must have thought I was with the police. When I asked to see the manager, he just nodded. But not more than thirty seconds later, a huge black guy—and I mean at least 6'9″ and 300 pounds—came lumbering up to me.

"I'm the manager," he announced. "What can I do for you?"

I took a deep breath and began. "My name's Harry Caray," I said, "and I broadcast St. Louis Cardinals baseball. I'm in town doing the NIT basketball tournament. The Billikens game ended about an hour ago. I'll be very honest with you. I've always wanted to see Harlem, but I couldn't get anyone else to come with me. This is the only place up here I've ever heard of, and before I even go to the bar, I wanted to talk to you as the manager. If I'm going to get in any trouble here, tell me now. If I'm in any danger, I'll get in a cab and leave. Otherwise, I'd sure like to stick around and just observe what goes on."

He just looked at me, surprised as all get-out. Then he says, "Listen, friend. The only way you'll get in any trouble here is if you go askin' for it. Now we can make room for you here at the bar or you can go on back to the nightclub. Take your choice."

I told him that I wanted to go to the nightclub, and he told me to follow him. It was about twelve-thirty now, and the joint was jumping. He set me up at a nice, comfortable table, right by the dance floor. I was relaxing, minding my own business. And then suddenly he put four of the most beautiful women you've ever seen right next to me. But I never even turned and looked at them; I figured I was being tested somehow. I just sat there, sipped my scotch and soda, and got in a kind of meditative mood. I watched the people dancing and having a good time, and I really had a wonderful time by myself. I was having an enchanted evening in this new place, just watching life tango by.

After about two hours, the crowd was thinning out, and I was contemplating leaving, when the manager came up to me.

"Is everything okay?" he wanted to know.

"Just fine," I assured him. "Listen, I really appreciate this. If you're ever in St. Louis, call me. If you want tickets to a ball game, anything at all, just let me know."

"I've checked you out," he said when I was through. "I have my sources of information, and I know you're who you say you are. I'm kind of intrigued by your curiosity, and if you really want to see Harlem, I can take you and show it to you. I'll show you the *real* Harlem."

Needless to say, I jumped at the opportunity.

He told me to wait a few minutes and then he'd be by to get me. I settled my bill, and sure enough he came by and we were off.

Outside, he had a pink Cadillac Eldorado that reminded me of Sugar Ray Robinson's famous car. We got in, drove a few blocks, and then pulled up in front of a dark building on a side street.

"This is our first stop," he announced.

When we got out of the car, he saw me looking suspiciously at the building. There wasn't a light on in the place, or any other place, for that matter.

"Don't worry about it," he said. "Just walk up the steps. I'll be right behind you."

Let me tell you, I was plenty worried. It was so dark I couldn't see the next step. And this huge, ponderous man was walking right behind me, his footsteps reverberating like a bass drum. Now I knew what everyone had been warning me about. Now I knew why the cabbies thought I was nuts. This guy had set me up. He was going to knock me in the head, take off with my cash, and leave me for dead. I'm just about to say to this fellow, "Here, I have some cash, take it and let me go," when we came to the fourth-floor landing.

"Here's where we stop," he said. He leaned across my shoulder—I definitely flinched when he touched me—and rang a doorbell.

All of a sudden, the door swung open, and it was Mardi Gras. The darkness and dinginess disappeared as if by magic. A band was playing great jazz. People were dancing. Booze was flowing. It was a party like I'd hardly ever seen before. I had the time of my life. And I couldn't even pick up a check or leave a tip—they wouldn't hear of it.

We stayed in that place for a couple of drinks, then headed off for another after-hours club. We stayed at the second place for a couple of drinks, and headed off for yet another club. By dawn, we must have hit six or seven places, and each one was just as much fun as the last. Some were in the basement, some up long flights of stairs. But all of them were incredible.

The sun was coming up when he finally dropped me off back

at the Commodore. I was about to say good-bye, when he asked me to sit and listen to him for a minute.

"My friend, now you've seen Harlem," he intoned. "It used to be the greatest place in the world. Nothing but the carriage trade. But it isn't that way anymore. Now it's dangerous. I can understand why your friends cautioned you against coming. You probably should've listened to them. But you came along and you had a good gimmick, your curiosity. You got me interested at first, to be honest with you, by making me wonder whether or not you were the police.

"Then, when I found out who you were, I knew you were legit. I intentionally placed those four ladies next to you to see if you'd make a move or not. You didn't. That was a point in your favor. So I figured you deserved to see what you really wanted to see. And, pal, you've seen it. So now I suggest you do what your friends did. When one of them is as curious as you were, advise him against coming up there. Because he might not be as fortunate as you. Or his approach may not be as intriguing as yours was."

I never saw that man again. But I took his advice. I've never been back to Harlem. I don't know if the Baby Grand or all those other great places still exist. But I do know I'm glad I had the desire to go there and the luck to run into the right guy at the right place.

Luck and desire.

They got me a memorable night in Harlem. I wonder how many other white people can make the same comment.

RUNS   HITS   CHAPTER

0   0   12

 **I** went through three regimes of ownerships with the St. Louis Cardinals. Sam Breadon, the original owner, sold the club to Fred Saigh and Bob Hannigan, who in turn sold out to August A. Busch, Jr.—"Gussie" to almost everyone who ever met him.

Like most things when it comes to the men who own baseball teams, these transitions of power did not come easily.

Sam Breadon, when he owned the club, had $5 million in capital put aside to build a new ballpark. At the end of five years, you either have to declare reserve capital as normal income or you have to go ahead and spend it. When Breadon's five-year period was up, he was not ready to build that new ballpark. But he realized that if he didn't build it, the government was going to take about 90 percent of his $5 million.

Fred Saigh was a tax-law specialist. He apparently knew of this peculiar situation, so he went to Sam Breadon and proposed a scheme. Saigh would take over the cash that was in the reserve fund so Breadon wouldn't get hit with that 90-percent tax. Then Saigh would buy the team from Breadon with that money. Breadon wouldn't lose a penny. All he'd lose would be the St. Louis Cardinals.

Breadon liked the plan, but he didn't really know Saigh too well, so he wavered. He wasn't convinced the government would go along with the deal. Fred Saigh, being an exceptionally bright businessman, brought in Bob Hannigan, whom Breadon knew very well. Hannigan had been the postmaster general, a Democratic senator from Missouri, and he'd also been director of the IRS. His credentials were impeccable. If Hannigan was part of the deal, Sam Breadon decided he'd go along with it.

So Bob Hannigan became Fred Saigh's partner and co-owner of the Cardinals—putting up only ten thousand dollars. A year later, he sold his share for a million.

I don't know how much Saigh had to put up, but I know it wasn't much. He'd just figured out the right tax scheme at the right time.

I guess Fred Saigh knew about my luck-and-desire formula.

But several years later, Saigh got into a tax problem of his own. The other baseball owners immediately began applying pressure, trying to force Saigh to sell the team. Although he had taken to baseball the way a duck takes to water—he loved the game, he had fresh ideas; he had the potential to be a real force —Fred was too distracted with his pressing financial problems to resist the pressure coming from baseball's lords and masters (ultimately, in fact, the IRS investigation of Fred Saigh led to a conviction. He even spent time in jail). So, in February 1953, he agreed to sell the club to Anheuser-Busch, Inc.

When Saigh was having his problems, there was a lot of talk about the Cards leaving St. Louis to go to Houston. But once Gussie Busch took over, that talk ceased. It became clear that if St. Louis could support only one team—and it could—the team to leave would be the Browns, who were owned and operated by the inspired but underfinanced Bill Veeck.

The Cardinals' future loomed bright and prosperous.

After all, Gussie Busch, president of Anheuser-Busch, Inc., had great business acumen. And he certainly had plenty of money—Anheuser-Busch is the largest beer company in the world; it sells nearly twice as much brew as Miller, the second largest.

My future, on the other hand, didn't look nearly so rosy.

I was safe for 1953. Griesedieck Brothers had already made their deal to remain the exclusive broadcast sponsor of Cardinals baseball before Busch bought the club. But once that deal lapsed, it didn't seem too likely that Anheuser-Busch would retain a broadcaster who had, for so long, been so closely identified with their competitor.

There was one other problem, too.

The public-relations man for the Anheuser-Busch Brewery was a man named Al Fleishman. He had previously been publicity director for Bill Veeck's Browns, but had since formed his own agency, Fleishman-Hillard, and his biggest account was Anheuser-Busch. It still is, as a matter of fact.

Al Fleishman didn't like me.

Veeck, when trying to compete with the Cardinals' popularity, used to say, "If I could only get rid of Harry Caray, I could get rid of the Cardinals."

He meant, quite simply, that I was popular and that I was a good salesman for my team. I took it as a compliment.

But word had it that Fleishman, when he heard his boss's comment, said to Veeck, "I'll take care of Harry Caray. You take care of the Cardinals."

Well, Fleishman never had been able to take care of me, and

the Browns eventually had to move to Baltimore, where—under the leadership of Harry Dalton, Hank Peters, and Earl Weaver, as well as owners Jerry Hoffberger and Edward Bennett Williams —they became one of the most successful franchises in modern baseball.

But now Fleishman had another chance. He wanted *anybody* but Harry Caray to broadcast games for the St. Louis Cardinals and sell Anheuser-Busch beer.

Once again, I heard the big names being bandied about. Red Barber, Bill Stern, Mel Allen. They made a familiar litany. Fleishman made it clear that since the Cardinals were now owned by a nationally known company, they needed a nationally known broadcaster and spokesman.

But Al Fleishman, for all his self-proclaimed brilliance, didn't know one thing.

He didn't know that I was about to meet Gussie Busch.

The Cardinals were traveling north to Chicago for a series with the Cubs, and Gussie had hooked his private car onto the end of the train. Sitting up front in the first car, with the players, I was in the middle of a card game when a messenger came into the car and said that Mr. Busch wanted to see me. I finished the hand, then headed back to the private car for my audience.

Gussie was there with John Wilson, who was then executive vice-president of the brewery, and Dick Meyer, a beer-company vice-president who would later become general manager of the Cardinals.

We shook hands, exchanged greetings, and had a polite social conversation about baseball and mutual friends. We were just getting to know each other, when Gussie dropped his bomb-shell.

"We want you to continue to be our announcer," he said, much to my shock. "You've done a good job, and we'd like to have you back," he continued. "But you have to understand, that does not include anyone else who is working with you."

Gabby Street had died a couple of years earlier, and I was working now with another ex-catcher, Gus Mancuso, who had a long big-league career with the Cardinals, Giants, Cubs, Dodgers, and Phillies. Gus had been there a year and had done a good job.

"Gus has been outstanding," I told Gussie. "Won't you consider keeping him on?"

"Harry," Gussie said with typical honesty, "we might be making a mistake even keeping *you* on. I don't take kindly to the fact that you've sold Griesedieck Brothers for so long. We're willing to make an exception for you, but we won't do it for Mancuso."

I'd tried to help Gus and failed. That was all I could do.

"Now I'm assuming," Gussie continued, "that you'll get permission from Griesedieck Brothers so we can talk to you formally. If they have other plans for you or don't want to give their permission, I expect you to tell us, so we can make other arrangements."

"I can't conceive that they'd hold me back," I replied. And that was the truth. If they didn't have the Cardinals' broadcasts, there was no other baseball for them to sponsor, because Falstaff had the Browns tied up for another five years. It would serve no purpose for them to tie me up.

Now here I have to tell you one thing, because it illustrates what a class act Griesedieck Brothers was all the way.

Every year, around Christmastime, Griesedieck Brothers would give out bonuses. They usually gave me fifteen hundred dollars, which was always greatly appreciated. When I talked to them about going to work for Anheuser-Busch, not only did they wish me well and give me their permission, at the end of 1953, they still gave me a bonus. My contract had run out in

October; I didn't even work for them anymore! But Ray Peters, then the executive vice-president, called me up, asked me to come to their annual party, and after a few drinks and a lot of fun, he handed me a check—for five thousand dollars. "Thanks for everything," he told me. How many people do you know who would do something like that? I don't know many.

Anyway, Gussie and John Wilson, back in the railroad car, wanted to know what I was making. I told them, and they promised me a five-thousand-dollar raise. They also told me I could have a two-year contract, which delighted me.

We shook hands, and it was clear that the meeting was over.

"Do I take this to mean we have a deal?" I asked.

"We have a deal," Gussie said emphatically. "But you are to keep it quiet. I don't want anyone to know yet."

Naturally, I kept it quiet. Incredibly quiet. I didn't tell a living soul. No way was I going to risk letting this get out and jeopardize my standing with Gussie Busch. Besides, Al Fleishman was still going around telling people I was going to be replaced. Listening to these stories, knowing what I knew, gave me great enjoyment.

What I didn't know was that there was some truth to them.

It turned out that after he made his deal with me, Gussie, who had a real mercurial streak, had second thoughts. It bothered him even more than he thought it would that his announcer was going to be this Caray fellow, who, for nearly a decade, had been so closely identified with Griesedieck Brothers.

It began to eat away at Gussie—fueled, I'm sure, by Al Fleishman. Finally, he had to call a meeting to discuss the subject of Harry Caray.

"Why the hell do we have to get a guy from Griesedieck Brothers to do our broadcasts?" Gussie demanded. "Why don't we get someone else?"

Now Gussie, like so many top executives, was often surrounded by yes-men, fellows who liked to play up to his ego and tell him he was always right. John Wilson, thank goodness, was not one of those yes-men. Wilson stressed that there were a number of reasons why Anheuser-Busch couldn't get someone else when they started sponsoring Cardinal broadcasts in 1954.

The first reason, Wilson reminded Gussie, was that they already had a deal with me. But Gussie was able to brush that one off.

"Don't worry," he said. "I'd never back out of a deal. We can pay him for two years, just what we promised—but we don't have to let him go on the air, do we?"

Wilson kept arguing.

I was popular with the fans, he insisted. And after all, Anheuser-Busch didn't just own a brewery now, they owned a baseball team. And that team was supposed to draw crowds and succeed on its own. He was sure I'd help do that.

Gussie seemed to be a little swayed by that logic. And then Wilson hit him with the most important reason: The brewery had no research to show what its distributors thought, but he was sure they would want Harry Caray selling their beer.

Now this was something Gussie understood.

Wilson pressed forward. The distributors had the most to lose, he pointed out, if the public became disenchanted with Budweiser and sales slumped. They also had the most to win if the public was pleased by the sponsorship of the Cardinals and thus sales improved. He suggested that the brewery survey the wholesalers in the Cardinal territory—which included Missouri, southern Illinois, Oklahoma, Nebraska, Kansas, all the Southern states, and Texas—to see who *they* wanted as the Cardinals' announcer.

About one hundred copies of the questionnaire went out.

"As you know, Anheuser-Busch has purchased the St. Louis Cardinals," it read. "Looking ahead to next year, we will be the advertiser. Which one of these announcers do you think will best fit the Cardinal and Budweiser image?"

It then went on to list approximately thirty names, all of the top names in sportscasting at the time, including mine.

And when the final accounting was done, the distributors had favored Harry Caray by a margin of ten to one.

When Wilson showed the numbers to Gussie, he was suitably impressed. He agreed that I was his man—with one caveat. The first season, I was to do no commercials. Those duties, by Gussie's dictum, were to be the exclusive province of my new side-kick, Jack Buck, who had come to St. Louis from Rochester, where he had been broadcasting the games of the Cardinals Triple-A farm club. The third spot on the team was being saved for Joe Garagiola, who was finishing his big-league career that summer of 1954 with the Cubs and Giants. Once he was done playing, Joe was going to join up with me. Gussie was determined that the public would have time to forget that I ever had anything to do with Griesedieck Brothers beer.

At first, everything went along as planned. I got along with my new partner, and to make it even better, Gussie and I really hit it off. Ultimately, this friendship may have helped my downfall with the Cardinals. I mean, here I was, not an executive or any kind of office power in the organization, but Gussie and I spent time together. We got along. We had fun. I'm sure this provoked a certain amount of jealousy and bad feelings from people who wanted to have—but didn't have—this kind of relationship with him.

Gussie Busch was my kind of guy, what I call a booze-and-broads man. He liked to have a drink, appreciate the qualities of a beautiful woman, tell a few stories, and play a few hands of cards. No pretense. No bull. For all his money and prominence —which is considerable; last time I looked, the Forbes 500 had him right near the top of the list—Gussie has always been a basic, down-to-earth person.

But as I said, he had a mercurial streak. One day, about a month into the 1954 season, we were playing cards when suddenly Gussie looked up from his hand and stared at me with a half-angry, half-quizzical expression on his face.

"Goddammit, how come you're not doing any commercials?" he asked. "What the hell do you think we hired you for, anyway?"

I was slightly taken aback.

"Jeez, Mr. Busch," I said, "you instructed me yourself not to do any Budweiser commercials for at least the first season. Don't you remember?"

"I said that? That's wrong, that's wrong," he muttered. "We want you selling our beer! That's what we hired you for!"

When it came to selling that beer, Gussie knew what he was doing. Getting involved so directly with baseball helped to boost Budweiser's image, not just in St. Louis but elsewhere. I don't know if you could prove it statistically, but I really do believe that Anheuser-Busch's association with the Cardinals and, later, its sponsorship of so many other teams' broadcasts, is largely responsible for its preeminence in the business. In 1953, when Busch bought the ball club, Bud was the number-two beer in national sales, trailing Schlitz by a considerable margin. By 1957, Anheuser-Busch was number one. It's never looked back.

But as much as Gussie knew about selling beer, running a ball club was a whole new experience.

Shortly after he bought the club, Gussie asked at a board meeting if there was anyone there who knew anything about baseball. Executive vice president Dick Meyer happened to casually mention that he had been a catcher for the Concordia Seminary team. And that was all that Gussie needed. "Well, then, you're running the team," he announced.

Between 1930 and 1952, the Cardinals played in seven World Series and won five. They managed a winning percentage above .600 eleven times. And they lost more games than they won only twice. In the first decade Gussie owned the club, it lost more games than it won five times, finished in the second division of the National League six times, and did not so much as play in the World Series, let alone win one.

In his excellent biography of Branch Rickey, baseball historian Murray Polner wrote of Busch:

"His fiefdom was run from his 281-acre estate, Grant's Farm, on the edge of the city where Ulysses S. Grant once resided before Lincoln chose him as his general. There Busch and his family lived in a thirty-four-room French Renaissance manor house set in a park stocked with exotic animals and through which the lord often passed on coach-and-fours, landaus, phaetons, or Russian sleighs. The question was: If Busch knew everything there was to know about the beer business, what in fact did he know about baseball?"

For a lot of years, many people asked that same question. Some of them were guys who were jealous of the friendship and rapport that Gussie and I had developed. So, too often, their answer to that question went something like, "He knows what Harry Caray tells him."

Well, to be frank, that was a lot of bull. Gussie and I rarely talked about baseball. Ours was not a business relationship, it was social. Usually, the closest we came to conducting business was when we were in a saloon together and we'd go behind the bar to serve drinks—trying to convince the owner that he should stock his place with Budweiser.

If Gussie came out and asked me a baseball question, I would give him a straight answer. But I would never raise the subject myself. When we were together, the conversation would most often be about politics or women or show business or marriage, this last being an endeavor at which neither of us excelled.

Inevitably, of course, we did have a few interesting conversations about the game.

Gussie was impulsive, no question about that. I'll never forget, one night we were having a drink at the Chase-Park Plaza and Gussie turned to me—a bolt out of the blue—and said that he was thinking of firing Bing Devine, who was on one of his many tours of duty in the Cardinals' front office. I never did understand why Gussie didn't really like Bing, who was a very likable man. Believe it or not, it may have been because Bing didn't smoke or drink or chase around after women. In baseball circles, those virtues are oftentimes considered weaknesses. After surprising me with his reference to Devine's firing, Gussie proceeded to truly shock me.

"Harry," he said, "how about you becoming my general manager?"

I almost swallowed my glass.

"You've got to be kidding," I told him.

He wasn't.

"Hey," he prodded, "you've been in baseball all your life. You know a lot about the players, the teams. Why *couldn't* you be my general manager?"

I didn't even stop to think it over.

"No," I told him.

He got a little upset. He was used to getting his way. "Give me one good reason."

"First of all, I'd have to take a cut in pay," I told him.

Gussie laughed heartily.

"Second of all, I'd wind up getting fired," I said.

He laughed again.

"Forget about all this stuff, Gussie," I told him seriously now. "You ought to get yourself a real good, solid baseball man, so you don't have to even think about your baseball operation."

"Who do you think I should get?"

This was one of the few times I did not regret being asked a baseball question by Gussie.

"Bill Veeck," I responded without hesitation, surprising my-self as much as I surprised Gussie. "He's colorful, he's a great baseball man, there's a small clique of Brownie fans still left in this town, and they drink beer, too, you know. Why *not* Bill Veeck?"

"You know," Gus said slowly, "it might not be such a bad idea at that. Do you know how to get hold of him?"

I told him I could probably find a way, and Gussie asked if I'd get right on it. Kind of excited now, I said that I would.

When I got home that night, I called Bill DeWitt, who was running the Cincinnati ball club then. Bill had been Veeck's partner with the Browns, and when I told him why I wanted to reach Veeck, he said he thought it was a sensational idea. He gave me Bill Veeck's phone number in eastern Maryland.

My next call was to Veeck himself. I told him Gussie was interested in having him run the ball club.

"Well, Harry," Bill said in his genteel manner, "you thank Gussie very much for me. But I've always had a policy that I wouldn't have anything to do with any ball club that I didn't own the biggest percentage of, or at least have the controlling interest in."

I told Bill that the Cardinals were owned by the brewery—in this case the stockholders—and that I wasn't sure something like that could be worked out.

"I don't know, either," Veeck said. "But thank Gussie for me all the same."

The next morning I reported back to Gussie. He considered Veeck's request and shook his head.

"I don't know how the hell I can make him an owner," Gussie pondered, mirroring what I'd said the night before. "Our shareholders own the club, and I don't think I can give any of it away to anybody."

He couldn't, of course.

And Bill Veeck never did make a triumphant return to St. Louis. I sure wish he had. He was just what Gussie Busch needed.

But many years later, Veeck and I did have a chance to work together in Chicago, and I think most people will tell you, we put on one heck of a show.

There were other occasions on which Gussie got me involved in serious discussions about the Cardinal management.

One involved the very same Bing Devine. Only this time, he was coming instead of going.

Gussie had invited five or six couples out to Grant's Farm for an elegant little black-tie dinner party.

I was there with my second wife, Marian. The other guests included Mark Eagleton, whose son, Tom, became a United States senator; Al Fleishman, my old nemesis; Bob Bascowitz, whose company produced all the glass bottles for Anheuser-Busch; and Tony Buford, a member of the brewery's board and its main lobbyist.

Now Gussie had just fired Frank Lane, who was famous for his many trades, and had brought Devine back as general manager. All night, over this wonderful dinner, Gussie was trying to get me to talk about it. And all night, I was avoiding the subject. At one point, I finally told him as emphatically as I could, "Gussie, let's don't talk about baseball tonight. There's no point."

"Dammit, Harry, I want you to give me an answer," Gussie said. "Did I make a mistake firing Frank Lane or not?"

"Gussie," I said impatiently, "all right! You keep insisting, so I'll tell you. And I assume you want me to tell you the truth, not just what you want to hear."

"That's right," Gussie nodded. "Just answer the question. Answer it any way you want."

I could see that his nerves were getting a bit frayed, too.

"Okay. If you're asking me, here's what I think. Bing Devine was a capable executive. You decided he wasn't, so you fired him. You hired Frank Lane. You didn't like him either, so you bring back Bing. The only way I can answer you is this way: Bing Devine cannot carry Frank Lane's jockstrap!"

With that, an eerie silence fell over the table. You could hear a pin drop.

Then Tony Buford's wife turned to Trudy Busch, who was Gussie's wife at the time, and broke the silence with a stage whisper. Leaning over toward Trudy, she mouthed, "Gussie ought to fire that son of a bitch."

Because of the silence at the tables, her whisper sounded about as subtle as a shout.

In one hell of an upset, my wife, Marian, stood up, pointed at Buford's wife, and actually took my side of an argument.

"Did you call my husband a son of a bitch?" she demanded. I was astonished. It wasn't as if Marian hadn't used the same phrase to describe me herself on occasion.

Buford's wife mumbled something about how she was talking about the yard man at Grant's Farm, and the dinner proceeded in even more awkward silence. All this, mind you, at a fancy black-tie affair.

Finally and mercifully, the dinner ended, and Gussie invited everyone into the den for drinks. On the way, Eagleton and Bascowitz came by to offer moral support.

"I admire your courage," Eagleton said. "But I don't know about your judgment."

Bascowitz whispered, "Harry, I hope the old man isn't mad. But he kept egging you on."

I told them both not to worry about it and suggested to Marian that she get her coat because it was time for us to leave.

Just as those words came out of my mouth, Gussie came walking up behind me.

"I heard you!" he yelled. "What're you saying about coats?"

"I'm going to leave, Gussie," I said. "I've had enough."

"Like hell you're going to leave! You're going to stay and play cards. I want some of your money." Then he threw his arm around me and he walked me toward the den, whispering the whole way.

"You son of a bitch," he murmured. "If you hadn't answered like that, I'd have fired you."

Later I found out what had precipitated the whole thing. When Gussie fired Lane and hired Devine, Fleishman had told him I had been a big supporter of Lane's but that now I would jump on the Devine bandwagon—just to cater to Busch. Gussie was out to prove to Al Fleishman that I was my own man— whether my opinions went along with the party line or not. My response proved him right, even if it did make for an uncomfortable dinner.

But that wasn't half as uncomfortable as I felt when Gussie got me embroiled in another one of his great baseball notions.

This one occurred in the middle of August 1964. The Cardinals were not in the pennant race. This was at a point in the season, in fact, when there wasn't a pennant race. The Phillies were running away with the National League flag that summer, and no one had any idea at all that they would take one of the most famous dives in baseball history and collapse like a lame horse in September. That no one included Gussie Busch, who was growing very impatient with his quiet, soft-spoken manager, a fellow by the name of Johnny Keane, whom I liked tremendously.

The Dodgers were in town one afternoon, and I struck up a conversation with Leo Durocher, then Walter Alston's third-base coach, around the batting cage.

This was when Gene Mauch was managing the Phillies, Eddie Stanky was managing the White Sox, and Alvin Dark was managing the Giants. They were all Leo's protégés. They were known as Leo's Young Lions.

I asked Leo if he still had an exclusive contract with NBC, which he always had said prevented him from going on local programs. He said no, so I immediately invited him to come on my pregame show. He hesitated, but I explained that I'd already talked to every player several times. I also told him that he still had a lot of fans in St. Louis—he'd played shortstop for the legendary Gashouse Gang team.

Finally, Leo said okay, he'd go on.

I should have smelled a rat.

Now, on this hot, muggy August afternoon, who should be sitting out at Grant's Farm listening to his radio but Gussie Busch.

So when I'm interviewing Durocher—about the Young Lions, about the Dodgers' pennant chances—I have to say,

"Look, Leo. How can you be happy just being a coach? You're a number-one man. You should be *managing* a major-league club."

"Well," he says, "I'm ready to become a manager again. I've had an obligation to Walter O'Malley and Buzzie Bavasi, who stuck with me after the commissioner suspended me. But I think I've met that obligation by now. I could've managed the Cleveland ball club, but that fell apart because I wanted a piece of the ownership. I'll tell you, though, if somebody came to me and asked me to manage a team with some talent on it—*a team like the Cardinals here*—well, I'd jump at it in a minute. Because a club like the Cardinals should be winning."

Well, Gussie, listening on the radio, didn't have to be prodded with a red-hot poker.

By the time I got up to the broadcasting booth to do the game, people there were practically hysterical. I had to call Gussie Busch! they said. Immediately! Use the hot line!

I picked up the phone, reached Gussie, and, of course, I knew what he was going to say.

"You've got to bring Durocher out here," he said. "Nine-thirty tomorrow morning."

"Gussie," I said, "you've got chauffeurs and limousines. *You* pick him up."

"No, no. This is an order," he said. "That's all there is to it!"

And, boom, he hung up the phone.

The game started a minute after that, and I, of course, had to do the broadcast. When it was all over and I was driving home, I suddenly realized that I'd totally forgotten about Durocher. I hadn't even told him about the meeting Gussie wanted.

When I got home, I called the people I knew Durocher was

friendly with in St. Louis—there were only three—and before too long, I was able to reach him. When I did, I explained the situation. Gussie had to see him. It was urgent.

At nine o'clock the next morning, I picked him up on a quiet side street near where he was staying. I drove him out to Grant's Farm, and we got there just as Gussie was sitting down to breakfast. He asked me to join them, but I didn't want to. I didn't want any part of this conversation. I *liked* Johnny Keane.

I just got back in my car and, as instructed, returned in about an hour. Gussie and Leo were sitting out front, obviously finished with their discussion.

Gussie insisted on pulling me off to the side.

"Look, Harry," he said, "if we make a change, Leo's going to be my new manager."

Swell.

When I got back in the car, I attempted to discourage Leo from discussing his deal with Gussie.

"I like Johnny Keane, and I don't want to get involved," I started out.

But I had about as much luck with him as I'd had with Gussie. All the way back, he was telling me that if Keane was let go, he was going to be named manager of the Cardinals. And all the time he was telling me this, he just wanted to know one thing.

"Do you think," Leo asked me ten times if he asked me once, "I can get a beer distributorship like Frank's got?"

He was talking about Sinatra.

And here's where the story gets crazier and crazier.

Before Gussie could hire Durocher, he felt he had to get Walter O'Malley's permission. Not only did Durocher work for O'Malley, the Dodgers sold Budweiser exclusively in their stadium. Gussie didn't want to rock the boat.

Walter was out of town, on some African safari, and couldn't be reached. So Gussie had to wait. If O'Malley hadn't been in Africa, Leo might have gotten the job.

Now while Gussie was waiting, here's where everything stood:

It was late August when all this started, and the Cards were mired in fifth place. Busch figured yet another season was going to pass without a pennant. He'd already fired Bing Devine as his general manager. The only reason he hadn't fired Keane before this was that it would have been bad form to fire both his general manager and field manager in the middle of the same season. But Durocher was the Billy Martin of his day—colorful, aggressive, successful. He was too good to pass up.

Meanwhile, in the American League—and this is crucial to the story—the Yankees were trailing the Orioles and the White Sox. Ralph Houk, who had been rewarded for winning three straight pennants by being promoted from field manager to general manager, did not think much of the job Yogi Berra was doing as his successor. Berra's tenuous position was made even weaker when he and Phil Linz, a utility infielder, had a much-publicized dispute over Linz's right to play a harmonica on a team bus after a particularly painful loss.

And as Gussie *kept* waiting, here's how things progressed:

One of Bing Devine's last trades was to peddle a washed-up pitcher, Ernie Broglio, to Chicago for a young outfielder named Lou Brock. It was one of the greatest trades in the history of baseball. Brock, who would eventually make the Hall of Fame, was just the spark the Cardinals needed. They started to win.

The Phillies collapsed. They lost ten consecutive games in the last two weeks of the season, blowing a six-and-a-half game lead. The whole season was coming down to the final weekend when the Phils were playing the Reds and the Cards were playing the lowly Mets.

Word got back to Johnny Keane that Durocher had met with Busch. He decided that the best defense was a good offense. Bill Bergesch was Ralph Houk's assistant with the Yankees, and Bergesch had been the general manager at Omaha, in the minor leagues, when Keane managed there. He was a big fan of Keane's ability, so he and Houk came to St. Louis—under assumed names—and met with Keane in mid-September. A couple of weeks after the Durocher story had leaked out, Keane signed a secret deal to take over as manager of the Yankees in 1965.

The Yankees, meanwhile, were making the greatest comeback in their history, managed by the beloved Yogi Berra—even though Berra, without his knowledge, had already been fired!

It was insane.

About this time, Gussie Busch realized what a truly excellent job Johnny Keane had done. He wanted to reward him with a contract extension—which, of course, Keane couldn't accept. Gussie kept after him, but Johnny kept putting him off.

"It's too distracting," he'd tell Gussie vaguely. "I have a pennant to win. There's plenty of time to talk contract."

Now it all came down to the final weekend. The Phillies are playing the Reds, while the lowly Mets are coming into St. Louis.

The first night, little Al Jackson beat Bob Gibson and shut out the Cards 1–0. The Phillies lost again in Cincinnati.

The next day, the Mets won again, 15–5. And again the Phillies lost.

Now the Reds and Cards were tied. If the Reds won on Sunday and the Cardinals lost, the Reds would win the pennant. The Phils, one game back, had to hope for a victory and a Cardinal loss. Then there'd be a play-off.

It was an incredible final day.

The Cardinals won and, of course, won the pennant when the Phillies finally managed to win a game.

And who were the St. Louis Cardinals going to meet in the World Series? None other than the New York Yankees, managed by Yogi Berra.

Somewhere in there, there had to be a conflict of interest. But you sure couldn't find one from the way the two teams played on the field. It was a close, hard-fought seven-game series, which the Cards finally pulled out, four games to three.

It was Gussie Busch's first World Championship. But he didn't have long to enjoy it.

The day after the Cardinals won, Gussie called a press conference. He wanted to announce that he was giving a new long-term contract to Johnny Keane. He wanted to tell the world that Johnny could write his own ticket.

The Board of Directors' Room at the Anheuser-Busch brewery was packed. Reporters were there from all over the country. Television cameras were rolling. And Johnny Keane was nowhere to be seen.

Gussie, Dick Meyer, and I were waiting for Johnny in Busch's office. Finally, about fifteen minutes after the press conference was scheduled to begin, Keane came strolling into Gussie's office.

Gussie shook his hand and started out the door. Keane hesitated.

"Come on, they're waiting for us and we're late," Gussie said.

Keane handed Busch a letter. Gussie put it in his pocket without reading it, and started to leave again.

"I think you better read that before we go in there," Keane suggested.

"Let's go, let's go. I'll read it later."

But Keane held firm. "I think you'd better take a look."

"Let me see that letter," Meyer now said. He grabbed it out

of Gussie's pocket, ripped open the envelope, and read it. All color drained from his face.

"We can't go in there," Meyer mumbled.

"Why not?" Gussie wanted to know.

"He's not going to manage," Meyer rasped. "He's resigning."

"You can't do that!" Gussie thundered to Keane. "We've got a press conference in there!"

"I'm sorry, Mr. Busch," Keane apologized softly. Then, in the understatement of the year, he said, "I've made other plans."

So they all had to troop in there, and announce that, instead of agreeing to a long-term contract, Johnny Keane, who had just won the first World Series for the St. Louis Cardinals since 1946, was resigning as their manager.

It was one weird scene, but it probably wasn't half as weird as what was going on in New York.

The Cardinals, at least, didn't fire Johnny Keane. He resigned. And the Cardinals could save face by replacing him with a beloved local hero, which they did.

The Yankees, though, were really stuck. They were forced to fire Berra—one of the greatest and most beloved players in history and a pennant winner as a rookie manager—and replace him with some guy no one in New York had ever heard of eight weeks earlier.

The Yankees had been praying that Keane would call them and say something like, "Look, your guy won. Thanks for the interest, but let's forget about our deal."

No such luck, of course. Because above all, Johnny Keane was an honorable man, who believed his word was his bond. To this day, I'm convinced he did not want to go to New York and the Yankees. He wanted to stay in St. Louis. But he'd made a deal, and he would never back out of it.

Believe it or not, there's yet one more irony to this whole mess.

At home that night, after Keane's resignation, I got a phone call from Red Schoendienst.

Red inquired after my health, asked me to explain the day's events, and then wanted to know if I had followed up on a conversation we had had back in July.

In that conversation, Red, who had been a great second baseman for the Cardinals and was now one of their coaches, told me that the organization wanted him to go to the minor leagues and learn how to manage. Red wanted me to tell Gussie that he had no desire to return to the minor leagues, had no ambitions to manage, and that he'd much rather spend the next twenty-five years as a coach. He didn't care about managing. He wanted security.

Now Red was asking me again if I had passed the word along to Gussie.

I told him I hadn't. As I've mentioned, I didn't like to get involved in Gussie Busch's baseball problems. But before hanging up, I did tell Red I'd try to mention it.

"Red," I warned with a laugh, "if you keep your nose clean with all the craziness that's going on here, *you're* going to wind up being manager of this club."

Of course that's exactly what happened. Gussie felt compelled to do something that would have a strong public-relations effect. And who better than Red Schoendienst? It was a perfect marriage. This was not a club that needed Durocher's "Nice guys finish last" attitude. Red had just the right touch for all the great Cardinals of that era—Bob Gibson, Curt Flood, Lou Brock, Orlando Cepeda, Julian Javier, Mike Shannon, Tim McCarver, Dal Maxvill, Roger Maris, and the rest. He kept them playing hard and playing together. Red won pennants in

1967 and 1968, and held on to the job he didn't want longer than any manager in Cardinal history—twelve consecutive seasons.

In difficult circumstances, Red Schoendienst, the reluctant manager, made Gussie look good. And for that he has been rewarded. Today, as a coach under Whitey Herzog, he has the job he always wanted and the security he always craved; Gussie has made sure he can stay as long as he cares to.

Gussie Busch is just a hell of a guy. He is capable of great loyalty and kindness, especially toward members of his Cardinal family.

I'm sure Red Schoendienst will surely be with the team as long as Gussie is.

And with Mike Shannon, it's the same thing. Mike is now one of the Cardinal broadcasters. When he came up as a player, he was loaded with talent, a terrific prospect. But then, while he was still quite young, he developed a kidney ailment and wasn't able to play anymore. Gussie put him in the booth, where he's been ever since, and he, too, can stay as long as he likes.

Gussie never forgets his friends. That's something I learned about firsthand.

On Saturday, November 3, 1968, I had just finished broadcasting a University of Missouri football game in Columbia, about a two-hour drive from St. Louis. While I was driving home, I heard the hockey game about to start. I figured it was going to be a perfect day. I'd go over to the arena, catch some of the hockey game, and then call a friend for dinner. So that's what I did. After the first period, I called a friend to meet me.

We went out to a nice dinner, and afterward decided to go over to the Chase-Park Plaza Hotel for a nightcap.

Now it was raining that night, really coming down. I drove over to the hotel, began to pull off Kingshighway into the driveway, and was all ready to turn my car over to the parking attendant. But because of the rain, I couldn't even get near the hotel. Traffic was backed up so far it looked as if it would take forever to reach the front door.

I backed out of the long driveway and got lucky. In my rearview mirror, I noticed there was a parking space right across the street, directly opposite the entrance. I pulled into the spot, tucked my yellow raincoat around me for protection, and started to cross the street.

That's when I was hit.

My friend heard the thud, watched me go sailing through the air, and I am positive I heard someone crying out, "Holy cow!" as I went flying by.

The driver—who had just returned from a tour of duty in Vietnam and who had gotten engaged to be married that very afternoon—knocked me about forty feet in the air.

I was lying in the street in front of the hotel, in the pouring rain. People started to gather around. Many recognized me; all were afraid to touch me.

A Goodwill truck came down Kingshighway. The driver saw a body in the street and, not knowing who I was, stopped his truck. When he saw I was just lying unattended to in the rain, he pulled a few burlap bags from the back of the truck and covered me with them—keeping me warm and dry—then just drove away. I think he saved my life.

When I finally woke up, it was the following Thursday, and I didn't know what the hell was going on. I looked around this room I had never seen before, and I felt awful. I figured I must have had a hell of a hangover. Then my nurse came in and told me I was in Barnes Hospital. Then I saw the casts on my legs.

"What the hell is going on?" I cried. She told me not to get excited, and then she explained what had happened.

In short, and without going into too many gory details, I had almost died on the street when the rainwater and blood nearly congested my lungs, and I was extremely fortunate they didn't have to amputate my left leg during surgery. As it was, I had two broken legs, a broken shoulder, and a broken nose.

The doctor then came in and told me I would have to spend quite a while in the hospital, that I would probably be there until Christmas.

Now most people would have let something like that interfere with their social calendar. But I wasn't about to. It was bad enough I was going to miss work—I was doing Missouri football over KMOX, my daily radio spot, and some basketball on television at the time—but I sure didn't want to miss out on any fun.

My room became headquarters for off-duty nurses, for kids who wanted to talk baseball, for all my friends. At night they would send martinis down from the restaurant on the top floor, as well as specially prepared meals, so I didn't have to eat the awful hospital food. After a while, it was like a nightclub in there. It got so I hated to leave.

Almost.

Just before Christmas, they decided to release me. I was estranged from my second wife at the time. That's when I found out what a good and kind man Gussie Busch is. He gave me his beach house in St. Petersburg, Florida, so I'd have a comfortable place to recuperate. He arranged for a private plane to fly me there. And he made sure there was a male nurse on duty twenty-four hours a day to care for me.

I won't say the recovery period was fun, but without Gussie Busch, it would have been a lot worse.

As it was, I managed to keep myself entertained. I had a lot of friends down there, and they were always coming by the house or taking me out to restaurants. I could get around in a collapsible wheelchair.

In February, I returned to St. Louis for a checkup. Because I'd been doing my isometric exercises so religiously—tightening my legs and relaxing them; tightening, then relaxing—I was sure the doctors were going to remove my casts. They told me I was making remarkable progress for a man my age, but they were only going to replace my big, heavy casts with smaller ones. I fought them. My legs felt strong, and I wanted to advance to crutches. I insisted. They were dubious, but reluctantly agreed.

I returned to Florida. Spring training was about to start, and I was determined to get myself in shape right along with the players. I worked hard, kept on with leg exercises, and by the end of spring training I had advanced from crutches to canes to the point where I didn't really need anything to help me walk.

I'll never forget that one day we were playing an exhibition game with the Cincinnati Reds. Dave Bristol was their manager then. Now, on the same day in November that I'd been hit by the car, a promising young outfielder named Hal McRae, only nineteen years old, had broken a leg playing winter ball in Puerto Rico.

I was on the field—still using crutches—and was hobbling along, going around saying hello to various players. Hal McRae —only nineteen, mind you—still had his leg in a cast. When Dave Bristol saw me, he called his team off the field and pointed his finger at me.

"Look at that," he said. "There's an old man. Broke two legs. Broke his shoulder. Broke his everything. And here he is walking around doing his job, doing anything he wants." He then turned to McRae. "Here you are, all you did was break your leg sliding into second base, and you can't get your leg out of your goddam cast! You ought to be ashamed of yourself."

Hal McRae, who told me this story years later, said it was one of the best motivational speeches he'd ever heard. He learned that he had to *want* to recover before he'd really be able to. McRae also said that every time he sees me to this day, he thinks, There's the guy who got me the greatest chewing out of my life.

Anyway, we came north to open the season in St. Louis. And as always on opening day, I was scheduled to function as the master of ceremonies. My job was to introduce the players and various dignitaries in attendance from a microphone stationed at home plate.

I don't know what gave me the idea, but I decided to give the festivities a little more life than they usually had.

With fifty thousand people crammed into new Busch Stadium, I came hobbling out of the Cardinals' dugout—hobbling along rather pathetically on two canes.

The fans gave me a nice, polite hand.

As I approached the first-base line, I knew I had them. I could feel their sympathy.

So I whirled one cane over my head and flung it as far as I could. Fifty thousand people cheered at once.

Then, using the other cane, I started hobbling again, toward home plate. Just before I got there, I stopped and looked up at the crowd. It was like a burlesque show.

"Throw it away!" they were yelling. "Throw it away!"

The second cane went flying.

It landed a good twenty to thirty yards away. Fifty thousand people went collectively crazy.

After the ceremony was over, I went into the dugout and was

about to leave for the broadcast booth, when Bob Gibson grabbed me.

"Harry," he said quizzically, "what the hell was that all about? You haven't used those canes for a week now!"

I just looked at him, and said, "Hey, Gibby, it's like I've always told you, pal. This isn't just baseball, it's show biz."

And you know, I wish that were something more baseball people realized.

Look at the Chicago Bears football team. William "the Refrigerator" Perry, the Super Bowl Shuffle, Jim McMahon's whole bit with his headbands—it's show biz. And it's marvelous. Because not only do they win, they entertain. They're showmen. And I think that everyone in sports management—the owners and the other decision makers—have to look at the job Mike Ditka did and say, "Is my team as entertaining? Is my manager or coach letting his team show its true personality?"

Owners and managers tend to treat their players like kids. Heck, these guys aren't kids, they're grown men! You can't give them curfews and order them not to drink beer on an airplane. What that does is take away their personality. And if you take away their personality, you take away their appeal.

What the hell would baseball be without the Babe Ruths and the Dizzy Deans? If you take the characters out of the game, you take the *character* out of the game.

And speaking of characters going out of the game . . .

Who knew that my act of bravado at the opening-day ceremony was going to be my last big hurrah in St. Louis, Missouri, after twenty-five years in the sportlight? Who knew that was going to be my curtain call?

But six months later, of course, I found out that show biz did not necessarily count for all that much in St. Louis.

After twenty-five years, after all we had been through together, they had an executive call me one afternoon in a saloon and tell me I had been fired.

And the next baseball voice I heard belonged to one Charles O. Finley. He said the O stood for "owner." Others said it stood for "outrageous." I figured I was just going to have to find out firsthand.

RUNS   HITS   CHAPTER

0   0   13

I wasn't out of work a month when Charlie Finley, the owner of the Oakland A's, called.

I'd known Charlie, talked to him many times; he'd even been my guest on the air. I'd always liked him.

At first the conversation was just the usual pleasantries. He kidded me about the various rumors that led to my St. Louis exile, wanted to know what I was up to.

I told him the truth; I hadn't been up to much.

Oh, I'd gone to the World Series that year. And everyone knows there are only two reasons a baseball man goes to the World Series: If he's *got* a job there, or if he's *looking* for a job there.

But I wasn't really looking too hard.

Times had changed since my days of sending out brash letters and résumés. I was pretty secure in the knowledge that someone would want me and come after me.

Well, Charlie Finley came to the dance.

"I want you to come up to Chicago and meet with me," he said over the telephone. "I can use a guy like you out in Oakland. You can put some fannies in the seats."

Finley lived in Chicago, where his enormous insurance business was located. He ran his baseball team by telephone and remote control, although a lot of his employees felt that it wasn't remote enough.

A few days later, I was sitting with Finley in his office at 310 South Michigan Avenue in Chicago.

It didn't take me five minutes to learn one very important lesson.

For twenty-five years, I had been one truly terrible businessman.

Charlie's opening offer to me was five years at seventy-five thousand dollars a season. It seemed like a fortune. This was, you must remember, in November of 1969. This was before double-digit inflation. This was before free agency.

I was pretty sure Finley had just offered to pay me more than he was paying any of his ballplayers.

I was certain he had just offered to pay me $27,500 a year more than I had made—as an institution—in St. Louis. In my last season with the Cardinals, I had been paid $47,500. I never argued about salary, to tell you the truth. I just signed for whatever they wanted to give me.

But I wasn't sure I was going to take Charlie's offer, as good as it was.

The money was terrific, but I didn't really need it. I was pretty well off by this time. And I was cocky enough to believe I'd get plenty of job offers. I'd already had several feelers. And I didn't particularly want to make a five-year commitment to live in Oakland. My roots were in the Midwest. As much as I loved traveling around the country, I had never lived anywhere else.

Also, my family was in St. Louis—Marian and the two daughters we had together, Elizabeth and Michelle. Now even though our marriage had its problems, I was still trying to save it at the time.

And finally, there was Charles O. Finley himself. He had made a favorable impression on me—and I have always tried to judge people by how they relate to me personally. But Charlie had a reputation for being impossible to work for. Getting tied up with him for five years did not necessarily seem like the smart thing to do.

I was quite sure, even though I went to Chicago for the meeting, that I was not going to take the job. And I explained my reservations to Finley.

He said he couldn't do anything about my roots or my domestic difficulties, but he could address the other issues. He sweetened the deal by throwing in a penthouse apartment on Lake Merritt and a Cadillac that I could use out there—I only had to pay for the gas. He offered to go from a five-year deal down to a three-year deal. That three-year pact shows, again, what a sharp businessman Charlie Finley was.

He had three more years coming in his contract with Atlantic Refining. They were the sponsors for the A's broadcasts. It was a tremendous contract—a million dollars a year for the rights, plus a hefty fee for the right to advertise on the stadium scoreboard, *plus* up to $150,000 that he could use to pay an announcer. If I'd known all this at the time, I could have held out for more. Basically, Charlie was getting me for free. None of my salary came out of his pocket.

I still didn't want to make a long-term commitment, but finally Charlie said he was willing to make the deal for one year. At the end of that year, we would evaluate the situation and see if we wanted to continue.

This idea intrigued me. How could I turn it down? For one year, I couldn't lose. I'd make good money, I'd spend time in the Bay Area—one of my favorite places—and I'd get to watch a team I knew was loaded with young talent.

I had only one more reservation.

Monte Moore had been the A's number-one announcer for several years. I didn't know how he'd feel taking a backseat to me.

Finley didn't anticipate any problems. Monte, he promised, would not make one penny less because I was coming aboard. When we were on radio only, Charlie wanted me to do play-by-play of the first three innings and the last three innings, as well as any extra innings. When we were televising, the arrangement would be exactly the same. Monte, he said, would be getting plenty of exposure.

It was clear that Charlie really wanted me. Every time I raised a question that could have been a deal-breaker, he had a ready answer. Every time I expressed any qualms, he soothed them.

After a few days of thinking it over, I ran out of excuses. I called Charlie and told him I would take the one-year deal.

But there was still one thing I was uneasy about—the quality of the baseball.

You see, for twenty-five years—hell, probably for fifty years—I had been brainwashed. I really believed that the brand of ball played in the National League was far superior to that played in the American League. And I really believed that watching the Cardinals was essential to my enjoyment of the game.

I honestly thought that my enthusiasm, the life I put into my broadcasts, was there because I was describing the exploits of my beloved Cardinals, because I was so familiar with their history and their great stars.

My year in Oakland showed me that these beliefs were foolish and unfounded. It was an illusion.

Because it isn't the city that you love. It isn't the team. It's not the names of the players or their personalities that keep you coming back day after day.

It's the game!

The game goes on forever.

Baseball is the object of your affections.

The uniforms are merely wardrobe. The players are just temporary actors on the stage. But the game keeps going on and on and on. It keeps on growing, getting better. The game is like a great play, like something written by Shakespeare. It is eternal; as long as someone with talent is playing Othello, the message and emotion are there. Not only was I able to switch from the Cards to the A's, from the National League to the American League, I learned that I could probably do a *Little League* game with the same kind of pride and enthusiasm that I do my major-league broadcasts.

Of course, the young Oakland A's made it easy to love the game of baseball. The team was on the verge of becoming one of the great dynasties in the history of the game. They hadn't yet won even a divisional title—that would not happen until the following season, 1971—but it was clear that summer that I was witnessing greatness, that there was something very special about that ball club. I couldn't know that between 1971 and 1975 the A's would win the American League West title five times and the World Series three times, but I could sense that something extraordinary was happening.

Reggie Jackson did not have a particularly good season in 1970. He and Finley engaged in a vicious contract dispute, and Reggie missed spring training. His home-run output fell from forty-seven in 1969 to twenty-three in 1970. Still, you could have written a prospectus offering stock in the man. It was clear that he had the potential to become the greatest clutch player and power hitter of his baseball generation. He could run and field, too. People don't remember, but Reggie had a great arm out there in right field. Not only was he a gifted athlete, but he was a bright and articulate man. He has never had the highest salary in the game, but I would venture to say he is richer than any other player. I would be willing to bet that he becomes the first former player to own a team.

I'll tell you something else about Reggie: I like and respect him. He played hard, and he understood the value of public relations. He put something back into the game.

Years later, when he was playing for Baltimore, I was in with the White Sox for a series. During the game that night, Ken Brett, a White Sox pitcher, threw a pitch up and in. It moved Reggie back off the plate, but there was nothing vicious or mean-spirited about it. It was just part of the game.

Well, Reggie got a little upset. He stood at the plate angrily jawing at Brett. Then he settled down, and the rest of his time at bat went without another problem.

In the ninth inning, off the same pitcher, Reggie hit a grand-slam home run to win the game. But instead of running the bases and celebrating the win, he stood at home plate yelling things out to Brett on the mound, embarrassing and humiliating him.

I thought it was bush, and later that night I told Reggie so. I saw him at the bar of the Cross Keys Hotel—where the White Sox stayed and where Reggie lived—and I went up to him.

"That was a cheap thing to do, Reggie," I said. "You made the pitcher look bad, you made yourself look bad, you made the game look bad. It was embarrassing for everybody."

"He was throwing at me," Reggie insisted. And he began to make a whole bunch of excuses.

"Don't give me that," I responded. "He wasn't throwing at you. It was a good, fair pitch, and you know it. You made a mistake and you should admit it."

Reggie didn't admit it, at least not that night. But he sought me out the next day.

"I was really bothered by what you said," he told me. "I thought about it all night. You're right, I did make a mistake. Let me go on your pregame show later and apologize."

And that's what he did. He apologized to the White Sox and to the people of Baltimore and the people of Chicago. He explained that he'd lost his temper, but that there was no excuse for it.

I thought it took a real man to do that. And that's what I think Reggie Jackson is—a real man.

Reggie, of course, was not the only great young star. In center-field, there was Rick Monday, who was a complete, finished ballplayer even in his early twenties. Joe Rudi was one of the most underrated players of his time; he was a great clutch player, offensively and defensively. Sal Bando played third just as well as Ken Boyer ever had. Bert Campaneris was one of the best shortstops I had ever seen. And Dick Green was so smooth at second.

Then there was the pitching staff. Catfish Hunter, just twenty-four years old, was already the mainstay. He won eighteen games that summer. Blue Moon Odom and Rollie Fingers were starting to make an impact. And at the end of the season, a shy twenty-year-old kid from Louisiana named Vida Blue came up from the minor leagues, pitched thirty-nine innings, struck out thirty-five batters, and won two games. The Oakland A's were a coming powerhouse.

Charlie Finley, of course, deserved as much credit as the players did. The guy was remarkable. He ran the ball club out of a briefcase in Chicago. He had almost no front-office staff, and very few scouts. He was a tightwad of the first order. But he beat all the great baseball men, all the men who had devoted their lives and their careers to the sport, at their own game.

He was able to do that because he was an incredible brain-picker. He would pick up the phone and call Buzzy Bavasi or Al Campanis or Bing Devine or some other baseball man just to shoot the breeze, and in the course of that casual conversation he would ask an essential question and come away with an important bit of information. He'd bide his time, but eventually he'd hear the same bit of information from someone else. Then from someone else. And then Charlie would figure it must be true. And no one was ever the wiser.

Charlie was street-smart. He would see his opportunities and take them, and worry about the questions of etiquette later. Hell, that's how he made his millions in the first place.

He was laid up in a hospital in Indiana, a young steelworker with a bum back and no future. One day, a doctor came into his room and tried to cheer him up. "Charlie, you've got to look at the bright side. You're in a union. At least you've got health insurance. Me, I'm a doctor. I've got nothing. We can't even *get* health insurance."

That got Charlie to thinking. He decided there was a fortune to be made providing health insurance to doctors. So when he got out of the hospital, he researched the insurance business and devised a plan. A few short years later, he had made that fortune. He was worth millions of dollars.

As you can tell, I respected Charlie. And I liked him. Much to everyone's surprise, we got along. In part, that was because

I never felt as if I needed Charlie. In part, that was because he was rarely around.

One time, though, he came to Oakland, called me at the apartment, and asked if he could come up for a visit. I didn't hesitate to say yes. It was, after all, his apartment.

When he got there, he said he needed to make a few phone calls. I offered to leave, but he wouldn't hear of it.

"I want you to listen to this," he insisted. "Stay."

Then Charlie picked up the phone and called Billy Martin, who had recently been fired as manager of the Minnesota Twins. Charlie wanted to discuss the possibility of Martin's becoming the manager of the A's. The conversation was quite serious. It got to the point where Billy asked about bringing his own coaches. Charlie said he would be delighted to have Mickey Mantle and Whitey Ford in A's uniforms. They talked about money and even came to an agreement. I'm listening to the whole thing.

Johnny McNamara was the current A's manager. He was a local boy, from Sacramento. That was his first season managing in the majors, but he'd managed a lot of the young A's down in the minor leagues, in Birmingham. He'd been doing a good job that year—the A's were running a close second.

Charlie had obviously begun thinking that if he had a more experienced manager, the A's might actually sneak in and win the whole thing, steal the division title.

Now I've always said that if I owned a team, the first person I would hire is Billy Martin. He's a winner, pure and simple. To my mind, he is the best manager in the game, bar none.

As I was thinking about all this, I heard Charlie, still on the phone, say, "This sounds good, Billy. But I've got one important thing to do before we go any further. Let me get back to you." Then he hung up.

"What do you think?" he asked me.

I told him what I thought—McNamara was doing a terrific job but he was learning on the spot; Martin could make the difference of three or four games that just might give the A's the title. Charlie agreed.

Now the important thing that Charlie had to do—as he'd told Billy—was to close a deal he'd been working on to buy Oakland's National Hockey League team, the California Golden Seals. Charlie's application still had to be approved by the NHL board of governors.

As we talked, Charlie somehow convinced himself that if he hired Billy, he'd lose the hockey club. Not because of Billy's reputation, but because he didn't think the NHL owners would approve of him firing McNamara.

After a couple of hours of going back and forth, Charlie called Martin to say he couldn't make the change.

Billy thanked Finley for his interest and hired on, as you might recall, first with Detroit, then Texas, then the New York Yankees, before he ever got back to Oakland. John McNamara kept his job until the end of the season. And Finley, much to his eventual regret, wound up with that hockey team.

Looking back, though, it is sort of interesting to imagine what might have occurred if Martin had hooked up with a twenty-four-year-old Reggie Jackson back in Oakland during the middle of the 1970 season.

One person Finley did make a meaningful job offer to that summer was me.

I had adapted quite nicely to my new surroundings. I enjoyed the climate and beauty of northern California. I discovered that the people there liked to have a good time the same way they did everywhere else. Jack London Square on the Oakland water-front was just as fine a place as I had ever found to have a cocktail and pass the time and appreciate the sights. I became quite a fixture there. Even after all these years, I bet that if I walked through Jack London Square tomorrow, somebody would invite me to have a drink just as if I'd never left.

One night, I walked into the Elegant Farmer, my headquarters on the Square. George Martinovich, the owner, told me that Charlie was in the back and wanted to see me.

I made my way over to Charlie's booth, and he invited me to sit down. As soon as I did, he went to work.

"You know," Finley observed, "one of my problems is that I'm an absentee owner. You're making an awful lot of friends here. I appreciate that. It's important, it's going to benefit our ball club. So I've just had a marvelous idea. I know you're concerned about roots and your family and security. Well, what if, in addition to your broadcasting deal, you came to work for the ball club? Year round. You could keep an eye on things for me."

I didn't know what to say. Luckily, I didn't have to say much, because Charlie kept talking. "I'll give you a three-hundred-thousand dollar loan, interest-free, to build or buy a home," he said, "whatever you want to do with it."

Stunned, I told Charlie how generous his offer was. I said that, of course, I'd have to consider it. The temptation to say yes was great, but I wanted to speak to my attorney.

The next morning, I called my lawyer in St. Louis and laid out Charlie's offer. He didn't think twice.

"It sounds great," he enthused. "You don't even have to build the home. Get the three-hundred-thousand dollars interest-free, and you can rent a home. Invest the money, pay back the principle on schedule, and make money."

But still I didn't do it. I just didn't like the idea of a five-year commitment. I knew Charlie and I knew me. Somewhere along the line, our friendly relationship would deteriorate. It had to happen, just by the nature of the respective beasts. And when it did, I didn't want to be locked into a long-term contract, no matter how lucrative the terms.

So I persuaded myself to pass up Charlie Finley's rather incredible offer.

At the end of the season, I thanked him for everything and told him I was going to return to the Midwest and try to find a job closer to my home in St. Louis.

I had done pretty well in Oakland. I'd had an interesting experience, made a host of new friends, and, as I've recounted, learned several important lessons. For all that, I credit Charlie Finley.

My next stop, of course, wound up to be even more interesting.

Chicago.

My kind of town.

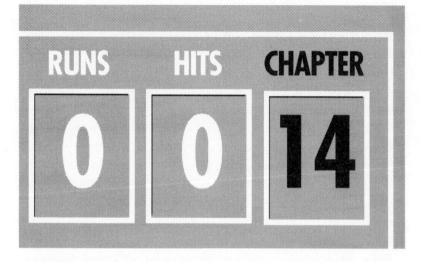

RUNS   HITS   **CHAPTER**

0   0   **14**

Once I was established in this business, I didn't really go after jobs. If someone wanted to hire me, I assumed he would call. That might have been a foolish assumption; in retrospect, it probably cost me the chance to work for a network, especially since Merle Jones, my first broadcasting benefactor, went on to be the number-three man at CBS, behind William Paley and Dr. Frank Stanton.

I don't have any real regrets about not going network, though of course you always wonder what might have been. I don't think I could have made more money. And I don't think I could have been any happier.

And I might not have gotten to live in Chicago, which has been one of the great pleasures of my life.

How I wound up in Chicago is a pretty interesting tale.

I went to the World Series in 1970—and I already told you

why baseball people go to the Series. I was letting the powers that be know I was available. It's the best possible place to advertise.

While I was there, I bumped into Jim Enright.

He had heard, he revealed, that Red Rush was going to be leaving as announcer for the Chicago White Sox and go to work for the A's. Jim had also heard that Rush had talked Charlie Finley into letting him bring Bob Elson along.

This really surprised me. Apparently, Elson was only going to do one inning a game, along with a pregame and postgame show. That was a strange twist. Elson had been the name announcer in Chicago; Rush had been the sidekick.

It seemed screwy to Enright, too. "You didn't have any trouble with Finley, did you?" he asked.

"No, no," I said. "Charlie was great to me. I just wanted to come back to the Midwest."

"Then why don't you call the White Sox? You'd be terrific for Chicago."

"I don't know," I said unsurely. "Chicago's my favorite town, but I don't know those people. I don't know that outfit at all."

"They're terrific," he insisted.

"Well, they know I'm available. If they want me, they can certainly find me."

"Whatever you want to do, Harry," Enright said. "But you really ought to think about it. Chicago's the place for you."

Now I went back to St. Louis, and I got a call from Pete Vonachen, in Peoria. He's a dear friend of mine, and now owns the Cubs' minor-league franchise in Peoria.

"You know," Pete started in, "Elson and Rush have left the White Sox. Holcomb's looking for a new guy, and you'd be great in Chicago."

I was starting to feel like a broken record.

"They know I'm available," I told Pete. "They know where to find me."

Without my knowing it, Pete, who knew Holcomb very well, called him up and sang my praises.

So a few days later, I got a call from Stu Holcomb.

Holcomb introduced himself—we'd met briefly a few times—and then got right to the point.

"I wonder if you could come up to Chicago. We'd love to work something out with you," he told me, "but I'd rather do it eye-to-eye."

"I'd be happy to," I replied. And made plans to go there the next day.

I got to the White Sox office about one o'clock in the afternoon. The girl at the desk told me that Mr. Holcomb was busy. Would I wait?

Of course I would. So I sat down.

What I didn't know was that Pete Vonachen had taken it upon himself to go to see Holcomb and tell him what he thought I could do for the White Sox. Holcomb, in fact, was listening to Pete at the very moment—without telling Pete that I was in the outer office. Holcomb might have thought the whole thing was a setup.

When Holcomb told the girl, "Send him in," I strolled into his office. Peter practically fainted. So did I. Holcomb, with a grin, said to Pete, "Now, if you'll excuse us, Harry and I have some business to discuss."

Vonachen delightedly stepped outside, and Holcomb and I proceeded to negotiate one of the most unusual contracts in the history of baseball.

The White Sox, Holcomb explained to me, were experiencing

hard times. Their owner was a guy named John Allyn, and they were strapped for cash. They were also a disaster on the field. The recently concluded season, 1970, had been the worst in the history of the franchise. They finished last, losing 106 games, and went through 3 managers. There was no star to speak of. And they had drawn just 495,355 brave and loyal customers— the worst year at the gate since the first year of World War II.

He made it sound as if broadcasting White Sox games was going to be more like joining the French Foreign Legion than playing the Palace. Which was all right with me. I appreciated honesty. I didn't need to listen to some phony recruiting pitch. I was just looking to make a deal. It struck me that things had to have bottomed out; there was nowhere to go but up, and I figured I could help improve matters. In a strange way, being the underdog appealed to me. Besides, they were trying to turn things around. They'd just hired Roland Hemond as their general manager, and a good young baseball man, Chuck Tanner, to be their manager.

Shooting straight, Holcomb admitted he couldn't pay me the kind of salary that Finley had, but he was willing to work out something creative that could earn me a great deal of money.

"You have a reputation for putting people in the seats, Harry," Holcomb said. "If you're willing to gamble with us, I think it might turn out pretty well. I'm not offering you a contract so much as I'm offering you a sporting proposition."

I was intrigued, and told him to keep talking.

"I can guarantee you a salary of fifty thousand dollars. Now I know that's less than Finley paid you," he began—I wasn't about to tell him it was also twenty-five hundred dollars more than the Cardinals had paid me in 1969—"but we'll pay you bonuses based on attendance."

Now I was really intrigued. "It's simple," he went on. "If *we* make a little money, *you* make a little money. If we make a *lot* of money, *you* make a lot of money."

This did not take me entirely by surprise. My reputation is that I put people in the stands. In a strange way, this approach struck me as kind of fair.

"We drew a little less than five hundred thousand last season," Holcomb continued. "We figure we ought to do better than that, so let's bump the number up to six hundred thousand. That's where you get involved. For every hundred thousand people you help us draw over six hundred thousand, I'll pay you ten thousand dollars."

Even before he'd finished talking, I'd already made up my mind that I was going to be broadcasting in Chicago. I stood up, stuck out my right hand, and told Stu Holcomb he had a deal. And a new announcer.

At first it wasn't easy to find an audience. You practically had to have military tracking equipment to pick up the White Sox radio signal, even if you were sitting in a box seat in Comiskey Park.

We didn't even have a station in Chicago. The AM flagship station of the White Sox radio network was WTAQ, a nice little 5,000-watt affair in the western suburb of LaGrange, Illinois. Believe it or not, our biggest audience was in St. Louis!

WGNU, a station in Alton, Illinois—across the river from St. Louis—picked up our broadcasts and, because of my popularity in St. Louis, broadcast the White Sox games back there.

Our big outlet in the city of Chicago, the second-largest city in the country, was an FM station that no one had ever heard of. When it wasn't carrying White Sox baseball, most of the programming was in Albanian. You know how to say "Holy cow!" in Albanian? Neither do I. And I didn't try to learn.

For a while, I wasn't sure there was anyone out there listening. Here I was talking about this greatly improved baseball team, giving optimistic reports about what a fine job this young Chuck Tanner was doing in his first full season as a major-league manager, here I was doing my damnedest to convince the people of Chicago that you really can't beat fun at the old ballpark, and I had the distinct impression I was talking to myself.

After the first few weeks of working on these tiny stations, one day, after a game, I stepped off the elevator at the Bards' Room level. When the elevator stopped, there was a group of people waiting.

Jack Drees, who handled the play-by-play on the telecasts over Channel 32, and I stepped out of the elevator together, right into the midst of the fans.

Now Jack Drees was 6'8", a former basketball star, a wonderful guy, an accomplished announcer, and he was on television damn near every night. He had been well known in Chicago for years.

I, on the other hand, was this little guy with glasses, on a radio network that catered specifically to those electrical engineers who knew how to find the signal. And I had been in Chicago for less than two months.

I figured I would bid Jack good night and head for Butch McGuire's, where there was a cocktail that had my name written all over it. Jack could stand there and sign autographs on his own.

But a funny thing happened. The people in the crowd ignored Jack Drees. It was me they wanted to talk to. It was me they were asking for autographs.

Harry, I said to myself for the first time, this might be your place, after all.

That 1971 season, Tanner worked a little miracle with a team that featured Bill Melton, Carlos May, and a baffling left-handed knuckleballer named Wilbur Wood. The team won seventy-nine games, and finished in third place.

Almost as important from my point of view, the White Sox drew 833,891 paying customers. Which meant I made an extra twenty thousand dollars.

The next season, we put together a radio network that was major league. Our flagship station was one of the biggest AM outlets in town, WMAQ, owned and operated by NBC. More important, however, the Sox added Richie Allen to their roster.

I'm sure when Stu Holcomb gave me the attendance clause in my contract, he didn't realize he'd have Richie Allen on his club.

When Allen entered the Chicago scene in the early seventies, he had several sensational years. He led the league in home runs, and won the MVP Award. He was a great drawing card as well as a great ballplayer. I'll be the first to admit that Richie Allen was far more responsible for the huge increase in attendance than I was.

If Allen had had the disposition of a Pete Rose or a Stan Musial, he might have been the greatest player who ever lived. In 1972, he was the first ballplayer ever to sign a quarter-million-dollar contract. And he earned every penny of it.

Yet he had a strange approach to the game. He was so good, he felt he didn't have to practice. Richie marched strictly to the tune of his own drummer. He showed up when he felt like it, took himself out of ball games when the mood struck him, took batting practice only when he got the urge. I was often critical of Chuck Tanner because of the way he handled Richie—with kid gloves. But upon reflection, at least he got some great years out of Richie. Perhaps if he'd tried to discipline him, Richie might not have been as productive.

In addition to Richie Allen, the White Sox hooked up with a new TV station—Channel 44—and I added television to my repertoire.

I had been doing TV since the early fifties in St. Louis, but never to this extent. With the Cardinals, we would telecast about thirty or forty road games a year, mostly Friday nights and Sunday afternoons. In Oakland, that one summer, we had a similar plan. But in Chicago we did about 140 games—we telecast every home game and about 60 road games. Mostly, we skipped night games from the West Coast; they started too late to attract and hold significant audiences.

From the beginning, from those first Spartan telecasts back in the early fifties, I had enjoyed doing television. It was liberating, although to tell you the truth, I don't think anyone has truly developed a TV style of announcing. I think most TV broadcasters are really doing radio broadcasts. I try to change my style a little bit for TV. The pictures speak for themselves, the essentials of the play are more apparent. I feel freer, as a TV announcer, to indulge in analysis, to provoke thought and argument. You can't let the camera do all the work. The people at home will get distracted if you do; they'll lose their concentration.

And now with the White Sox, I could do TV almost every day; as the number-one play-by-play man, I did the first three and the last three innings on television, and the middle three on radio.

All in all, it was one terrific package. The team improved to 87–67, finished second in the American League West, and attendance soared. The Sox drew 1,186,018, and my bonus was $50,000. That was it. That's where my deal ended.

The next year the product slipped, the team won only seventy-seven games and finished fifth. But my popularity continued to increase. Now let me go on record here.

I'm not one of these guys who thinks the announcer can *really* put people into the stands. I think the players put the people there. The success of the team is what fills the stadium. All that an announcer can do is make the broadcasts interesting enough so that the fans will want to keep following the team. An announcer can't *get* the fans interested. What he can do is *keep* the fans interested.

I try to create an atmosphere of fun. Like my expression, "You just can't beat fun at the old ballpark," I say it all the time and mean it. And I'm sure I convey that to the fans. With me, they'll sing; with me, they'll laugh. I can add to their enjoyment, and that's all I really want to do.

It's not such a big trick saying, "Ball one . . . strike one . . . Ball two . . ." Baseball's an easy game. It's not hard to pass the information along. There are shadings and nuances, sure, but the game itself is simple—simple to watch, simple to understand. Maybe that's why it's been so popular for so long.

That's why I say there's not a bad announcer in baseball. Some are just more interesting than others. To me, you can tell an uninteresting announcer—when he throws a million statistics at you. Who cares whether a player's got 120 singles or 140 singles? Or who cares if he's had two hits in his last twenty times at bat? I'd rather know that he's never had a hit off a particular pitcher—something that is actually relevant to what's happening on the field.

You know, there's been a phenomenal rise in the scrutiny paid to baseball statistics. Guys like Bill James and the Elias Bureau. But I may have been the first guy who was giving those kinds of statistics on the air. Way before it was popular—before Davey Johnson's computer or Earl Weaver's index cards—I used to keep those kinds of stats every day. I know that the last time Rusty Staub faced Bob Gibson, he went 0-for-4 and that during his career he'd been 1 out of 37. So when Staub came up to face Gibson, I was able to say factually, "Hey, he has trouble hitting this guy."

Now, they feed us a lot of statistics. Too many. I think the important ones are getting lost in a big pile of nothing.

Not only was I feeding statistics to the city of Chicago, my phrases were starting to seep in. Jack Brickhouse, who was the voice of the Cubs for four decades, had been the most beloved and discussed sportscaster in town. His trademark celebratory "Hey! Hey!" was ingrained in the vocabulary of every school kid in Chicago. But now I was beginning to have the same impact. The White Sox were starting to take over the town.

And if the way school kids talked didn't tell you that, White Sox attendance did. In 1973, the fifth-place Chicago White Sox, a team that was never a factor in the pennant race, attracted 1,316,527 paying customers, the fourth highest in club history.

All this while, I took up residence in the posh Ambassador East Hotel. I still live there, paying a monthly rental fee for my apartment. As my wife, Dutchie, enjoys reminding me, I've spent so much money there in the last sixteen or seventeen years that I could have bought the place by now.

But I don't intend to move. I've always liked it—I stayed there when the Cardinals or A's came to town. The Ambassador East, you see, is strategically located. It's a short walk from some of my favorite haunts. It's right in the strike zone of good living and good company.

The Pump Room is right in the hotel, just off the lobby. Half a block away are places like Yvette's and Turbo and P.S. Chicago and Hotsie Totsie. And my friend Butch McGuire, who was probably the originator of the singles bar, has a great place. And then there's Arnie's. And last but not least, as of October 24, 1987, there's a wonderful spot on 33 West Kinzie by the name of Harry Caray's.

I finally figured out—I told you I wasn't a real smart businessman—that after all the money I'd poured into other taverns and restaurants throughout the years, I might as well have a piece of my own. I'm very happy with Harry Caray's. We've got a great bar area, several dining areas, meeting rooms, and best of all, an outstanding menu with reasonably priced meals. If you don't believe me, you can come in yourself. The number is 312-H-O-L-Y-C-O-W. I spend quite a bit of time in there, particularly evenings after day games at Wrigley Field.

One other thing about Chicago. I remember one day in particular, when Tom Fitzpatrick, the Pulitzer Prize–winning columnist of the *Sun-Times,* decided he wanted to do a column about me. People were writing about me all the time in Chicago. Unlike in St. Louis, a tragedy didn't have to strike before I'd get mentioned in one of the Chicago newspapers.

Tom called me early one morning to see how we could work out an interview. I wasn't thrilled. I was nursing a hangover. But I also wasn't about to miss the opportunity for publicity, not when I was getting paid for selling tickets.

"Meet me at twelve-thirty in the Pump Room," I said, figuring I could manage that, as the Pump Room was right downstairs.

I arrived first, had a Bloody Mary, and determined that I needed to take some air. When Fitz arrived, I suggested we take a walk down to the Barclay Club, a private place of which I'm a member. It was only ten minutes away, and we could have lunch there.

We headed down State Street on this nippy, typical fall day, and we hadn't taken but a few steps when a mail truck pulled to a sudden stop.

"Hey, Harry," the guy driving the mail truck hollered, "good ball game last night."

I thanked him and kept going.

Then, about three steps later, a little old lady stopped us and asked for my autograph.

A couple of kids on bicycles skidded to a halt to talk baseball.

When we walked by a grocery store, the people who owned it came out and insisted on giving me some fruit to take home.

It was as if I had planned the assault to impress Fitzpatrick. I had to swear my innocence to him.

He was astonished. He was also taking careful notes.

"Does this go on all the time?" he wondered.

"Except when I'm sleeping," I had to admit.

By the time we got to the Barclay Club, I must have talked to three hundred people. Every five steps, we were mobbed. Girls crossed the street just to come over and say hello (which, of course, I didn't object to). Mothers had rushed to see, wheeling their baby carriages. Drivers had slammed on the brakes and jumped out of their cars to ask for autographs.

To me, it was all in a wonderful day's work. But Fitz couldn't get over it.

The next day, he wrote a column about what had happened; He didn't leave out a detail. It seemed as if he remembered every single word everyone said. And from that point on, my reputation as Chicago's Good Time Harry was pretty well established.

A couple of years later, I got my official title.

Jimmy Rittenberg is the owner of Faces, a private disco on Rush Street that has thrived and survived every fad for years. He also runs Ditka's, a popular restaurant built in association with the coach of the Bears, Mike Ditka. Rush Street was originally the nightclub capital of Chicago, and it's still one of the most dynamic streets in the country. That's where all the action is, which might be why Jimmy Rittenberg named me "the mayor of Rush Street."

I consider the title an honor.

Also, I intend to serve until the day I die.

RUNS   HITS   CHAPTER

0   0   15

The media has been good to me.

But every so often, a columnist in one of the road cities will write that I'm a homer.

This is about the poorest description I can possibly think of.

I am not a homer. Never have been. Never will be.

Sure, I want my team to win. I wanted the Cardinals to win. I wanted the A's to win. I wanted the White Sox to win. And now I want the Cubs to win. I want every Cub pitcher to win thirty games, and every Cub hitter to hit sixty home runs.

That's not being a homer. As I've said before, that's human nature. And it's part selfishness. The better my team does, the more attention I get. The more my value goes up with the ball club and the sponsor—because the ratings go up.

A homer, to me, is an announcer who tells you only half the story, the half he thinks the management of the club wants you to hear.

A homer sugar-coats.

He makes excuses for mistakes and errors and lousy play. He won't mention it if a player isn't hustling.

When I'm at that ballpark broadcasting a game, I'm the eyes and ears for that fan at home. If I don't tell that fan the truth, the whole truth, and nothing but the truth, he or she isn't going to hear it. And the fan deserves to hear it.

If I'm such a homer, why hasn't there been any other announcer in America whose job has been on the line so often? And it's always on the line for the same reason. One faction is always claiming I'm too critical. Either it's the owner of the team, or the general manager, or field manager, or the players, or some combination of the above.

Naturally, once these complaints begin, management has a decision to make. Does he stay or does he go? And this is why I always say I'm working for the fans. Eventually, if you tell the fans the truth, the fans will make it known that they want you to stay around. That's a tough vote for any owner to ignore.

Either my definition of "homer" is wrong, or these people who call me one are badly mistaken. Because if they only knew the troubles I've had . . .

I remember when Eddie Dyer was manager of the Cardinals, Fred Saigh decided, after the 1950 season, to fire Eddie. As I was about to go over to cover the press conference, Saigh called me up and asked me not to go. I took great offense when he told me that Dyer thought I was responsible for his ouster—he thought I'd criticized him too much on the air.

Ask Eddie Stanky if he thought I was a homer. Eddie was the nicest guy in the world as long as he wasn't wearing a baseball uniform. A loving family man, he attended mass every Sunday. But put him in uniform, and it was like Dr. Jekyll and Mr. Hyde. On the field, the guy became the most miserable so-and-so in the world. He would have run over his own mother to win a ball game.

Or ask Chuck Tanner. I consider Chuck a good friend and a great manager. Maybe he could be a little tougher, but who knows? If he were tougher, he might not be as good as he is. But Chuck Tanner didn't think I was a homer. He thought I did as much good for the White Sox as a truckload of sore arms and torn knee ligaments.

Chuck never understood what my job was.

For years, we had bitter ideological disputes. On airplanes and buses, in hotel bars and around the batting cage, he would explain his theories, and I would explain mine. Rarely, in five years, did we agree.

Chuck was something of a mother hen as a manager then. He thought it was his job to protect his players from the slings and arrows of criticism. He wanted to pump them up and tell everyone how great he was—even if he wasn't. And Chuck was absolutely convinced that it was the broadcaster's duty to assist him in this effort.

In short, Chuck Tanner wanted me to be a homer.

As you might imagine, I didn't quite agree with his philosophy.

I don't know how many times I explained it to him. But I did, over and over again.

"Your responsibility is to get the most out of your players," I'd spell out. "My responsibility is to get the most out of a broadcast. That means I have to tell the truth, and if I hurt the feelings of some of your ballplayers doing it, that's the way it goes."

One of the things Chuck never really understood, nor did many of his players, was my popularity. I'd try to explain that also.

"I'm going to be more identifiable than you," I used to say. "And people are going to be talking about me as much or more than they talk about you. They do that in any city about any announcer who's been around for a while or is doing any kind of job at all."

I do believe that to be true. An announcer is in everyone's home for three hours every day. We become almost a part of the family. Ballplayers, except for the biggest stars, aren't recognizable on the street because they look different in their civvies than they do in their uniforms. Their personalities don't have the time to develop as something familiar. People don't know what they sound like, or what, for the most part, their opinions are.

But people don't think the broadcaster is more important than the team. Clearly, he isn't. The team is what they come out to the ballpark to see. The team is who they want to see win. The broadcaster is just the guy who entertains them and serves as the liaison between them and the team when they can't come out to the ballpark.

In one form or another, I said all that to Chuck dozens of times. I hoped Chuck would understand. And I hoped he would explain things to his ballplayers when they complained about me.

It didn't happen that way.

Chuck, of course, managed the Pirates for many years, and then managed the Atlanta Braves until he got fired in the middle of the 1988 season. And guess who the announcer of the Braves is? None other than Skip Caray.

Skip's a little subtler than his old man. That's because he went to college. I always say that I'm a graduate of the School of Hard Knocks, while Skip's a man of letters from the University of Missouri. But at least Chuck couldn't completely escape the Caray family.

His players used to want to escape, as well. They kept using me as a scapegoat, taking out their frustration by blaming me for their failures.

One I remember in particular was Bill Melton. He was a pretty good third baseman who made the All-Star team once and led the club in home runs three years in a row. Melton is the club's all-time home-run champion, although it's with the not overly impressive career total of 154. He was a big, handsome fellow, and I liked him.

Anyway, one day on the air I said something critical about Melton. He'd made a baserunning error where he failed to advance, and it cost the team a run. It was a reasonable and accurate observation. It was also nothing extraordinary, and the kind of thing I would have forgotten about the next day.

Except the next day, Melton came storming up to me in the hotel lobby, made a big scene, called me all sorts of unpleasant names, and basically told me off in front of all his teammates and friends just before we got on the bus to go to the ballpark.

I suppose he thought he was acting like a big hero. I was pretty angry, but I held my tongue and waited until I could get him alone out on the field to find out what the problem was.

Once we got out there, I confronted him.

"Look, Billy," I explained. "I don't understand. Tell me what you're teed off about."

"I don't want to talk about it!" he snapped. He started to walk away, then turned back. He looked at me almost pleadingly. "Goddammit, you've always been on me. From the first day you got here."

Well, that was a lot of crap. He knew it and I knew it. I had actually been one of his biggest boosters.

When I went to work for the White Sox, I had pointed out to him that the year before he had hit thirty-three home runs and it had been baseball's best-kept secret. But if he hit thirty-three home runs when I was broadcasting, I promised everyone would know about it. If he kept playing as well as he had, I told him I would make him a lot of money.

And, by God, that's exactly what happened. He hit thirty-three homers again my first year in Chicago, and I let the world know about it. Bill Melton started getting national publicity. He also began making endorsement money he had never before seen.

But he didn't want to hear about that now, when things weren't going quite according to plan. By the time we had our argument, he'd developed a bad back. With the painful injury, his skills had deteriorated. The toughest thing for an athlete is to look in the mirror and say, "Gee, how could I be that bad?" They can't admit that they can't do something, that they might have made a bad play. So for the rest of his time with the White Sox, until he left the club in 1975, he blamed me for all his problems. He never talked to me again, either, after that explosion.

When our tiff became a big story in the Chicago newspapers, Tanner got into it and, naturally, took his player's side.

That ignited a public feud between Tanner and me, one that kept growing and growing.

Every time I said something the least bit critical about one of his players and he heard about it, Tanner would unload on me in the morning newspapers. Chuck had his ego, too. It was his team, and he wanted to prove he was in control. I guess it was his way of letting his players know that he loved them.

Chicago had four dailies at the time—the *Tribune* and the

Sun-Times in the morning, the *Daily News* and *Today* in the afternoon—and there was cutthroat competition on the baseball beat. So if Tanner had a quote in the morning papers, the guys from the afternoon papers would call me, and I would respond in kind.

It made for some lively reading.

It also made for some ridiculous nonsense.

One time, an infielder named Luis Alvarado lost a ball in the sun, and it dropped for a hit. I made some crack like, "Jeez, Luis grew up in Mexico. The way the sun shines down there, you'd think he'd be used to it by now, and never lose a ball in the sun."

It was innocuous. It was silly. It was the kind of thing intended to be forgotten a minute later. But the next day, there was Chuck making a big stink about how I had ridiculed Alvarado in public.

Another time, Bee Bee Richard, a kid shortstop, made three or four errors in the early innings. A couple of innings later, someone threw a bottle on the field and it shattered into a million pieces, which Bee Bee proceeded to clean up. "That's the first thing Bee Bee picked up cleanly all day," was what I said.

I went down to the clubhouse when the game was over and mentioned my comment to Bee Bee. He thought it was funny.

But Chuck made a federal case out of it.

Finally, it dawned on me that Chuck and I were giving our best stuff away. I figured we could do better than that.

So I went to the ballpark one afternoon, found Chuck, and told him there was no reason for us to sell newspapers when we needed to improve our television ratings. I told him that whenever he had something to say about my broadcasts, he could come on the pregame show and say whatever was on his mind. He did, the ratings went up, and though we still never agreed, we established a relationship of mutual trust and respect.

There was a happy ending to that story, and in time, there was a happy ending to the Melton story.

A couple of years ago, I ran into Bill in Anaheim. He was as pleasant as could be. He apologized for the trouble we had. He said he regretted our dispute. We had a drink and toasted better times.

Of course, Melton's biggest problem at the time was insecurity. He was afraid of losing his job, and he had the mistaken notion that somehow my commentary might cause that to happen.

That's usually how it happens. The superstar doesn't complain when you criticize him. And neither does the ambitious rookie. It's the fringe player who gets upset, the veteran who is nearing the end of the line. It seems as if those guys really believe that what an announcer says is going to determine whether they make it or not. They really believe that if an announcer doesn't mention the error they made or the time they struck out in the clutch, then maybe management won't notice and they'll be able to hang on a little longer.

Of course, a general manager doesn't need an announcer to tell him when a ballplayer is at the end of the line. It's right there out in the open for everyone to see, every day.

While all that is indisputably true, my run-ins with Tanner and Melton and a couple of other members of the wonderful White Sox family damn near cost me my job after the 1975 season.

The team had started losing again that year. Attendance declined precipitously—to 770,800 from 1.1 million in 1974. It seemed clear that the White Sox had reached the point of no return. And why not hop on the bandwagon—owner John Allyn decided that he would blame me for all his problems.

One night, I was home watching television. Channel 7. Dan

Devine, then the Notre Dame football coach and a very good friend of mine, was being interviewed. Unbeknown to me, Johnny Morris, on Channel 2, was interviewing Allyn. The shocking part of the interview was when Allyn, out of the blue, announced that if he returned as owner of the White Sox in 1976, one of the things he'd be sure to do would be to hire a new announcer. No more Harry Caray.

I didn't see any of this. I'm still watching Dan Devine, blissfully unaware of what's going on. But my phone rang almost immediately. It was Tom Fitzpatrick, who was then a sports columnist for the *Sun-Times*.

"Are you watching television?" he wants to know.

I told him I was.

"Well, what do you think?" he demanded.

"I agree with Devine. I think Notre Dame's going to have a hell of a team."

"What are you talking about? Aren't you watching John Allyn?"

"No," I said.

"Turn on Channel Two. You've just been fired."

Needless to say, I jumped for the TV set. But I was too late. The interview was over. But the phone rang again, almost instantly, and this time it was Johnny Morris. He told me he wanted to get my response to this rather surprising turn of events. He wanted me to come on his ten o'clock broadcast.

"You're the first to call," I said. "So you've got it."

Now the phone began to ring off the hook. Everyone wanted to know what was going on. I wasn't sure myself, though I had an idea.

I think Allyn knew he was going to sell the Sox, knew he wouldn't be returning in 1976. And I'm sure he wanted to go out a hero with Chuck Tanner and his players. What better way to make points than to say, basically, "See, fellas, if I'd been there, I would have gotten rid of Harry Caray."

Of course, that night I couldn't be sure Allyn wasn't going to return. All I could be sure of was that my job was on the line again.

The timing couldn't have been worse.

Just a few months earlier, I had had a feeler from Gussie Busch about returning to St. Louis to pick up where I had left off so suddenly six years earlier as the Cardinals' number-one play-by-play announcer.

Jack Buck had moved to NBC to start a show called *Grandstand*, which has evolved into, more or less, their current pregame show. When Jack announced that he was leaving, Gussie called me on the phone.

It so happened that my wife, Dutchie, was in the hospital in St. Louis, so I had already flown there that day to be with her. When I checked into my hotel, around eleven-thirty at night, there were several messages from Gussie Busch. He had tracked me down.

I didn't believe it. I figured somebody was having some fun with me. Especially because I didn't recognize the phone number. But I called anyway.

It turned out to be legit. The reason I didn't recognize the number was that he was at his hunting lodge, not his home.

I got through to Gussie. He'd been waiting for my call.

"Harry," he said, "I want you to come back to St. Louis."

"Forget it," I told him immediately. "St. Louis is yesterday for me. My future's in Chicago."

"Come out and see me," he insisted. "Maybe I can make it worth your while."

"I'd love to see you and talk, Gussie," I said. "But I won't take the job."

"Just come tomorrow," he said.

So I did.

I went out the next afternoon. I guess I was flattered that he wanted me back.

Gussie said that nothing would happen like what happened before—the crazy rumors, the internal politics, the firing.

The next thing he said was that I wasn't to say a word about our conversation. No one knew we were talking except for Bob Hyland—the head of KMOX—and Bing Devine—the Cardinals' general manager. Gussie then told me he'd invited his lawyer over. When the lawyer, whose name was Lou Sussman, arrived, he let it slip in conversation that he'd discussed my possible return with Al Fleishman. Remember, when Bill Veeck owned the Browns and said, "If we can get rid of Harry Caray, we can get rid of the Cardinals," Fleishman was the one who responded, "I'll take care of Harry Caray." Well, I hit the roof. So much for secrets and no internal politics.

So I told Gussie he could stop trying to woo me back. I just wasn't interested. By this time, I was convinced my life was meant to be lived in Chicago.

But now it looked as if I wouldn't be living in the employ of the White Sox. Not as long as John Allyn owned the club, anyway.

Luckily for me, he didn't own the team for too much longer.

On December 10, 1975, a group of investors led by Bill Veeck bought the Chicago White Sox.

My job was saved. Maybe.

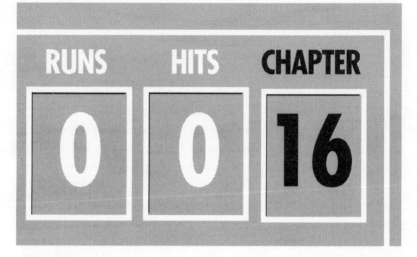

RUNS   HITS   CHAPTER

0   0   16

The Chicago public was thrilled that Bill Veeck was now owner of the White Sox. First and foremost, he certainly would keep the team in Chicago.

No one was happier than I was. Not because I thought Veeck was going to rehire me as a broadcaster. As a matter of fact, I had reason to believe just the opposite was the case. We'd had kind of a shaky history together, and I honestly felt he'd replace me.

The last time we lived in the same town—St. Louis—we had been competitors, rivals. Bill had been the owner of the Browns, and I had been the announcer for the Cardinals. And in the years since, he had blamed me for a lot of the troubles he had had in St. Louis.

In fact, in Bill's book, *Veeck—As in Wreck,* he even claimed I tried to prevent him from buying the Browns, which just wasn't true. He wrote that on my daily radio show, I had tried to persuade the Browns' fourteen hundred public stockholders to hold on to their stock rather than sell to Veeck—because he needed those shares to have full control.

Actually, what I said was something extemporaneous on a Cardinal broadcast. I had a friend, Bill Sulzer, who was a one-armed Western Union teletype operator at old Sportsman's Park and truly one of the most amazing people I'd ever met. Well, Bill had some stock in the Browns. So when the sale of the ball club was announced, I merely joked that maybe with Veeck owning the Browns, my good friend Bill Sulzer might make some money. That was it.

Things never came easy for Bill Veeck.

The owners certainly didn't want him to own the White Sox. They didn't like Veeck. He was too smart for them. He showed them up. Bill did things to add to the enjoyment of the fans at the ballpark, while the other owners did things to *take away* that enjoyment.

Then Commissioner Bowie Kuhn, the owners' mouthpiece, almost broke the White Sox deal. Kuhn decided, at the last instant, that Veeck and his coterie of investors didn't meet Kuhn's high financial standards. He told Veeck that if he wanted the deal to go through, Veeck would have to raise an extra one million dollars—in twenty-four hours.

Bill did it.

Nothing got in his way of owning a ball club.

Something was getting in the way of Veeck's hiring an announcer, however.

A couple of months passed, and I hadn't heard a word. Now I'm sure that, partly, this silence was intentional. As long as he didn't make a decision, the papers would write about us. Would Veeck hire Harry Caray? Whom would he hire instead? What's Harry going to do? It was great free publicity.

One evening, Bill and I both attended the Baseball Writers'

Association's big Diamond Dinner. During the banquet, it seemed as if every fan there was discussing my future.

At one point, when *Tribune* sports columnist Dave Condon, the master of ceremonies, was trying to make a presentation, the crowd spontaneously started cheering, to my tremendous embarrassment, "Har-ry! Har-ry!" One person in that crowd wasn't embarrassed: Bill Veeck. I don't know if that's when he decided to talk to me about the White Sox job, but I'm sure it helped. Because as they were chanting, Bill was sitting up on the dais with a big ear-to-ear grin. Bill saw that the public liked me—and Bill Veeck was a man who was more interested in success than in personalities or petty politics.

Shortly thereafter, he made his move. He invited me up to his suite at the Executive House Hotel for a meeting.

My appointment was for five-thirty. When I arrived, the door was open and a note was tacked on it.

Come in, it said, *I'm soaking my leg.*

Actually, to be precise, Veeck was soaking his stump. He had lost most of his right leg as a result of an injury suffered in World War II. I went into the room and shouted a greeting. A voice emanating from the bathroom told me to fix myself a drink and relax.

Twenty minutes and two drinks later, Veeck emerged from his tub and walked into the room.

For a moment, there was an awkward silence. I figured it was his room and his booze and his ball club, so he had first serve.

He didn't say hello. He didn't ask me how I was. He didn't tell me to drop dead. He didn't tell me to go to hell. He didn't shake hands.

He just looked me up and down, pursed his lips, took a puff on his cigarette, and said, "Well, well, well, if it isn't the man who ran me out of St. Louis."

I wasn't startled. I didn't even wait a beat. I just responded in kind.

"Bill, don't give me that bullshit," I said. "Gussie Busch and his millions had something to do with it."

We both had a good laugh.

Then we sat down, talked a little about Chicago, a little about baseball, a little about broadcasting, worked out a deal, and shook hands.

So began one of the most rewarding and fulfilling relationships of my years in baseball.

Of all the men I worked with and for in this game, I respected none more than Bill Veeck.

He understood with greater clarity and vision than anyone what the game was about and whom it was for. And he explained it very simply.

"Every day is Mardi Gras," he said. "And every fan's a king."

Bill devoted his life to that great notion.

As long as the game is played, Bill will be remembered as the man who sent Eddie Gaedel, a 3'7" midget, to bat in the Browns game in 1951.

But he should be remembered for so much more.

As a teenage employee of the Cubs, whose president was his father, Bill Sr., Veeck planted the ivy that still decorates the outfield walls of Wrigley Field. In that same capacity, he helped build the beautiful, graceful, and efficient manual scoreboard that still rises above the center-field bleachers in the little ballpark on Chicago's North Side.

Later, in 1959, when he had his first go-round as owner of the White Sox, Bill conceived and erected the exploding scoreboard that continues to celebrate hometown home runs with fireworks displays—annoying the neighbors but dazzling the fans at Comiskey Park on the South Side.

In between, he devised the season ticket, created Ladies' Day, established the first promotional giveaway days, and signed the first black player in American League history, Larry Doby.

And always he took care to make sure the ballparks were clean, the concession food was good, the popcorn smelled right, and the beer was cold.

He also won more often than he lost.

The Cleveland Indians won their last World Series in 1948, when Bill owned them. They also set an attendance record that stood for more than a decade.

The Browns didn't improve much on the field when Bill ran them, but they doubled their attendance, anyway.

And, of course, his first time around with the White Sox, they played in their only World Series since the Black Sox scandal of 1919.

So it was with great optimism that Bill pulled his MacArthur and made his triumphant return to Chicago in the months preceding the 1976 season.

It was with great and inspired joy that he went to work. The ballpark had suffered from neglect during the last years of the Allyn regime, so Bill immediately ordered it spruced up. He also improved the quality of the fare served at the concession stands, and he replaced the astroturf infield with real grass.

We all thought it would be only a matter of time before the White Sox were playing in the World Series again.

And then, just a couple of weeks after Bill's deal was finalized, an arbitrator named Peter Seitz ruled that baseball's reserve clause—the regulation that bound a player to his club forever and prevented free agency—was illegal.

Within months, it became clear that the economics of the game would be dramatically altered. Bill had bought a business in one world, and was going to have to operate it in another entirely. He never had a chance. He simply did not have the money or the backing to compete for players with the likes of George Steinbrenner and Gene Autry, Ted Turner and Gussie Busch.

But Veeck hustled and laughed and had a hell of a good time, anyway. He installed a shower in the center-field bleachers at Comiskey Park. He had a barber working on the premises. And Bill staged dozens of promotions, some of which backfired. I'll never forget that ill-fated "Disco Demolition Night" in 1979, when a "tribute" to old-fashioned rock 'n' roll turned into a near-riot and forced the White Sox to forfeit the second game of a doubleheader to the Detroit Tigers.

And one year—1977—he "rented" a couple of home-run hitters named Richie Zisk and Oscar Gamble (they came inexpensively in trades because they were veterans who would be free agents and sign with other teams at the end of the season) and almost stole a pennant when the team won ninety games and was in first place until August.

Still, it was always a struggle to stay solvent in those changing economic times. Money, not performance on the field, invariably had to be the first consideration.

For five years, Bill operated with blue smoke and mirrors. He continued to create the illusion of progress and maintain cause for optimism by frequently changing managers—going from Paul Richards to Bob Lemon to Larry Doby to Don Kessinger to Tony LaRussa in five seasons. Veeck never let the fans know his financial problems. He always kept in mind his guiding dictim.

Every day *was* Mardi Gras. And every fan *was* a king.

And no one enjoyed it more than I did.

Bill's mind was just absolutely magnificent. No one thought the way he did. No one could.

For instance, for as long as I could remember, ever since the first games I went to, I would sing along when the organist played "Take Me Out to the Ball Game." It was that way in St. Louis. It was that way in Oakland. It was that way the first five years in Chicago.

It was no big deal, but at every game, Nancy Faust, the talented organist at Comiskey Park, played the song during the seventh-inning stretch. And every game I would sing along, though the only people who could hear me were Jimmy Piersall and the TV producer.

On opening day in 1976, Bill's first day as owner, he noticed that some of the fans sitting just below the broadcast booth looked up, took the cue when I started singing, and sang along with me. It had been happening that way for years, but I'd never given it much thought. To me, it was just something that happened.

Bill didn't say anything, but he watched to see if the same thing kept occurring during the next few days. And, of course, it did.

His mind told him that the people were singing along because they could *hear* me—which was, in fact, the case, since they were near the booth—so Bill decided that we should share the fun.

He did not, however, mention a word to me.

He just had a public-address microphone installed secretly in the broadcast booth and had it turned on during the seventh-inning stretch.

Next thing I knew, my voice was booming over the public-address system, and thousands of people were singing along with Nancy and me.

After the game was over, I ran into Bill in the Bards' Room, which served as a press and staff dining room before games and a watering hole after games.

"What the hell was that all about?" I asked.

"Harry, I've been looking for a guy to do that for thirty years," Veeck said. "But I never could find the right guy before. Well . . . you're the right guy."

"Thanks," I said, puffing up with pride at what I thought was great flattery.

"Don't you know *why* you're the right guy?" Bill asked.

I thought I did, so I told him, "Sure."

But, clearly I didn't.

"Harry," Veeck went on, "anybody in the ballpark hearing you sing 'Take Me Out to the Ball Game' knows that he can sing as well as you can. Probably *better* than you can. So he or she sings along. Hell, if you had a good singing voice, you'd intimidate them, and *nobody* would join in."

Many years later, I'm as well known now for singing that song during the seventh-inning stretch as I am for shouting "Holy cow!" Proving the Great Veeck knew a lousy singing voice when he heard it.

Sometime during that same season, Bill had another promotional idea that excited me even more than singing. He proposed that the White Sox hire my oldest son, Skip, away from the Atlanta Braves. He wanted us to work together as the game's first father-and-son announcing team.

I was thrilled. Because if there was one thing I had done right as a father with any of my five kids, it was to get Skip started in broadcasting.

I was divorced when he was quite young. I didn't get to spend as much time as I would have liked with him, so I took Skip with me on the job, as often as possible. During school vacations, he came down to Florida for spring training. And during the season, he would hang around the ballpark for the first couple of innings of night games, before going home in time for bed. It even became something of a tradition for me to bid him good night on the air when it was time for him to turn off the light and go to sleep.

But by the time he was in high school, Skip hadn't shown any interest in going into broadcasting. Now every successful father I knew wanted his son to go into the family business. But I knew I shouldn't push Skip into something he didn't want; I realized instinctively that that would backfire. If I was too blatant in expressing my desire for him to consider a career in broadcasting, he would rebel and become something completely alien . . . like a doctor or a lawyer. So I deliberately stayed away from the subject.

But time was running out. Skip was sixteen years old then, a junior in high school, and I figured I'd have to do something devious if I was going to get him interested in what I considered to be the family business.

With this in mind, without saying a word to Skip, I took my good friend Bob Hyland, who ran KMOX, to lunch. It seemed fitting. Merle Jones, as general manager of KMOX, got me started on my career; many years later, his successor was about to help launch my son's career.

"Bob, I'll trade you an idea for a promise," I said.

"What is it?" he wanted to know, clearly intrigued.

"You've got every kind of sport on KMOX except high-school sports," I said. "I think it'd be great if one day a week, late Saturday afternoon, you'd devote a fifteen-minute show to high-school sports. It'd be tremendous," I enthused. "Every mother and father would be listening. Every kid who plays a sport would be listening. All their pals and girlfriends. There's a real audience here in St. Louis for that kind of thing."

"You're right," he agreed. "It's a good idea."

"Fine," I said, getting right to work. "Now here's the promise I want you to make. Skip does the program. And here's the way you make that happen. You call him up, tell him about the show, and ask him to provide you with some names of students at his school, Webster Groves High, who might be able to handle it. Then, no matter who he mentions, no matter what the qualifications, you reject that person. He'll never mention himself. He's too modest. And besides, he doesn't think he wants to be a broadcaster. So finally you tell him he's got to do you a favor. You tell him the show's already listed. The spots are already sold. And you really need someone in the studio Saturday at five-fifteen. You ask him to help you out just this one time and do the show. Then you'll call him back Monday and get some more names."

Hyland agreed to play along.

"Wait, I'm not done," I said. "When you call back Monday, you never mention the show. Just ask him for more names."

Hyland said that sounded okay, too. Now it was time to see if I really knew my boy.

The next thing I knew, Skip was calling me, all excited.

"You've got to be tuned in to KMOX at five-fifteen on Saturday," he crowed. "You're in for a big surprise."

"What the hell?" I feigned ignorance. "You going to be interviewed or something?"

"Just tune in," he said. "You'll see."

As soon as I hung up with Skip, I started calling everyone I knew in St. Louis. I told them I didn't care *what* they were doing, but at five-fifteen on Saturday they had to listen to him. At five-thirty, they had to call the station and tell him what a great job he did.

Saturday came along, and I listened to the show. It was fairly simple but fun and entertaining. Skip was terrific.

By previous arrangement, the first call to get through at five-thirty was from me.

"Boy, are you full of surprises," I enthused. "Man, oh, man, were you good. Holy cow, Skip, I didn't dream you could do a job like that."

After I hung up, the station received a deluge of phone calls.

As you might imagine, Skip was anxious to hear from Hyland on Monday. But when he called, Bob didn't deviate from the plan at all.

"Skip, thanks for helping me out of a jam," he said nonchalantly. "But have you thought of any more names, people I can consider?"

"Gee, Mr. Hyland, I've given you everyone I know," Skip replied.

Bob started to thank Skip again, and said he would call someone at another high school. He told him he had a good contact at Kirkwood, the big rival to Skip's school. Skip couldn't take it anymore.

"Mr. Hyland, did you listen to the program?" he asked.

"Sure, sure," Bob said.

"Well, what did you think?"

"It was fine, Skip. I knew you'd do a good job. But your dad told me you didn't want to become a sports announcer."

"Dad's wrong about that!" Skip said. "I never said that. Gee, Mr. Hyland, if you can't find anybody, I'd be happy to do it again this Saturday. And I'll be even better at it."

The con had worked. Skip was hooked on broadcasting. He worked again the next Saturday, and hasn't stopped since. He also hasn't needed any help from his old man since. He made it on his own all the way. From the University of Missouri radio station to minor-league baseball to St. Louis Hawks basketball to being the voice of the Atlanta Braves on Ted Turner's powerful superstation, Skip Caray has made it on his own and made his old man very proud. I might not have been the world's greatest parent, but I was very happy about how this little plan of mine turned out.

As I said, at one point Veeck offered a job to Skip to join me in the booth with the White Sox. But Skip, again doing things on his own, rejected it. At the time, I told him he was making a mistake, that Chicago was too big a market to pass up. But I probably was speaking more with my heart than my head. Skip did the right thing. He's never referred to as Harry Caray's "kid," nor should he be. Skip has carved a terrific niche and created a great following in Atlanta. He's become one of the most popular and respected sportscasters in the country.

My other children are doing fine too. Chris has a good job with an executive travel agency in St. Louis, Elizabeth is a building manager in Chicago, Michelle is a housewife in St. Louis, and Pat is doing the same in Atlanta. I've been very lucky that way too.

Anyway, because Skip didn't come to Chicago, I got to work with Jimmy Piersall on White Sox broadcasts, and we turned out to be a hell of a team.

I suppose I was responsible for getting Jimmy his job with the White Sox.

One year, I didn't have a regular partner in the booth. Every time we went into a city, we'd pick up a different ex-player to do the color alongside me.

Piersall was connected to the Texas Rangers, and we worked together down there. I thought he was terrific.

Jimmy had everything I look for in a broadcasting partner. He loved and knew the game. He was articulate, opinionated, and outspoken. Plus, he worked hard.

He had spent seventeen seasons in the big leagues—he played

with Ted Williams for the Red Sox and for Casey Stengel with the Mets—so he could speak with authority.

Jimmy was also just crazy enough to put up with me. I mean that, of course, literally. For all of his great accomplishments as a ballplayer—and there were many; I remember going in to Boston's Fenway Park and listening attentively while ushers pointed to places on the field and told me about all the great catches Jimmy had made—what he will always be remembered for is battling back from mental illness. Early in his career, Jimmy had a nervous breakdown and was institutionalized. But he didn't quit. He made it back to the big leagues and became an inspiration to many other Americans who were afflicted with mental illness. In fact, his story was so inspiring that it was first published as a book and then made into a movie, *Fear Strikes Out*, with Anthony Perkins starring as Jimmy.

Jimmy and I got along great together and put on a hell of a show for the audience. The players didn't always like it. Many of them thought we were too critical. And management didn't always like it, thinking we were making it difficult for them to sell the public on the players. But the fans responded. Jimmy always thought Bill Veeck didn't like him because once, when he was still a player, he had gotten fed up with the fireworks shooting into the air after a home run and threw baseballs at Veeck's beloved exploding scoreboard.

But White Sox baseball became more popular than ever on the Chicago airwaves, even though the team was losing.

Even the comedy troupe at Second City—the legendary improvisational workshop in Old Town that spawned Elaine May and Mike Nichols, Shelley Berman, John and Jim Belushi, Bill Murray, Brian Doyle-Murray, Gilda Radner, Betty Thomas, David Steinberg, and so many other great comedy stars—did a sketch taking off on the raucous way Jimmy and I broadcast baseball. In the sketch, I was played by George Wendt, who has since gone on to play Norm on the hit television show *Cheers*, and Jimmy was portrayed by Danny Breen, who is one of the stars of HBO's *Not Necessarily the News*.

Jimmy was so full of energy that broadcasting nine innings of baseball every day was not enough of an outlet for him. So he offered his services to the team as an unpaid outfield coach. Veeck, who recalled as well as anyone that Piersall had been one of the greatest defensive players of all time, accepted gladly.

For a time, Jimmy's coaching paid dividends. White Sox out-fielders started doing some strange and wonderful things. They threw to the right base. They hit the cutoff man. And they backed each other up. They stopped losing easy fly balls in the sun, and started to make diving catches the proper way—by getting their bodies in front of the ball, so if it bounced free it wouldn't roll to the wall while the opposition circled the bases.

But when Tony LaRussa became the manager, he objected to the way Jimmy criticized—however legitimately—the players during the broadcasts, and dismissed him as a coach. Jimmy was bitter about that, but he tried not to let it show.

For the next several days, everything was fine. On the air, it was the same as it had been for the previous couple of years. We'd talk about the ball game, and when things got a little slow, we'd start kidding around.

"Did you take your pills today?" I would ask if he got a little hyper about a play that didn't seem extraordinary.

And he would come back with the perfect response. "Hey, listen, I have papers to prove *I'm* sane. Do you have papers to prove *you're* sane?"

Then one evening, a couple of hours before a game, at the

time he would ordinarily have been coaching, I ran into Jimmy beneath the stands and noticed he seemed a little down. I figured I needed to do something to cheer him up.

I pointed out that the Sox had made eight or nine errors in the last couple of games, and that he got out just in time.

"Boy, oh, boy, you came out smelling like a rose," I said. "I'm already starting to get letters saying the White Sox wouldn't have made all those errors if they hadn't taken you off the field as a coach. But who the hell needs that coaching stuff, anyway? This way, you come to the ballpark, have a hot dog, read the papers, talk baseball, and go to work."

He agreed with me. His spirits seemed to improve. He then said he was going to the clubhouse to get a Coke and that he'd meet me later in the booth.

"Yeah, yeah," I kidded. "You'd rather walk all the way to the clubhouse just to get a Coke for free than turn around and buy one at the concession stand for fifty cents."

He laughed, and I thought everything was okay.

So I went down to the field to do the pregame interview show, then headed up to the booth for the broadcast.

But when I got there, Piersall was nowhere to be found. A few minutes later, someone came rushing in and told me to get to Veeck's office on the double.

Veeck was waiting for me, and he wasn't happy.

"You know what happened to your boy?" he asked. Bill always called Piersall my boy. "He's really done it this time. He just tried to strangle Bob Gallas."

Gallas was a sportswriter who covered the Sox for the *Daily Herald*, a suburban newspaper.

I was astonished. "When could this have happened? *What* could have happened? I just left him. He felt wonderful."

"Well," Bill said, *"something* happened."

Then Jimmy was brought into the office. He was crying, his body was shaking. It was awful.

"Jimmy, what the hell happened?" I asked.

He couldn't explain. He just kept saying he was sorry.

"I shouldn't have done it," he sobbed. "I don't know why I did it."

Veeck could have been angry. Most other owners certainly would have been. He could have fired Jimmy on the spot. Attacking one of the sportswriters so violently would have constituted just cause. It was clear that this was going to cause the ball club a great deal of grief.

But Bill never raised his voice. He just asked the doctors to take care of Jimmy and see that he got the proper medical treatment. Then he turned to me.

"Just go on the air and explain that you'll be working alone because Jimmy was taken ill," Veeck ordered. "That's all."

And that's all that Veeck ever made of it. Jimmy was on leave for a few weeks while he recuperated. Lou Brock took his place and worked with me. When he was healthy enough, Jimmy returned to the booth with Veeck's blessing.

For all the hoopla and all the hustle, Bill Veeck was a great humanitarian, a kind and decent man.

In fact, the only regret I have about our association is that I didn't get to know him better as a friend.

A couple of winters back, not long before he died, I ran into Bill at T.J.'s on the South Side.

"Bill, one thing I can't understand is why you and I weren't close friends," I admitted. "Our styles are the same, we like the same people, we like to have a beer, we like to talk, to argue. And yet we hardly ever associated. You'd say hello to me, I'd say hello to you. You'd say good-bye to me, I'd say good-bye to you. We went through five years together with the White Sox, and we were never together for more than five or ten minutes at a time unless there was some problem."

"Well," he said, "don't you know why?"

"No," I confessed. "Why?"

"Harry, if you and I had been real good friends, we would have gone places together," he said. "And we would have covered only half the territory. You went your way and sold the White Sox the way only you can do it, and I went my way, selling the White Sox as only I can do it. By not being together, we sold twice as much."

A brilliant man, Bill Veeck. And it's an absolute crime that he's not enshrined in baseball's Hall of Fame. If justice is done and he's inducted, it will be too late for Bill to enjoy it, unfortunately.

Bill Veeck died on January 2, 1986.

He wasn't my best friend. He was just a fellow I worked for, liked, and respected immensely.

We all are going to miss him very much.

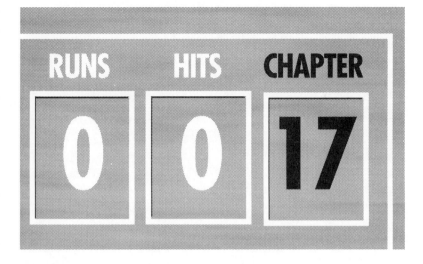

After five summers of swimming bravely against the cruel and powerful economic waters, Bill Veeck finally surrendered to the financial realities and put the White Sox up for sale at the conclusion of the 1980 season.

And the same fine human beings who made it damn near impossible for Veeck to buy the White Sox went out of their way to make it almost as difficult for him to sell.

What happened was fairly simple. After weeks of weighing offers and negotiating with a variety of potential buyers, Veeck and his partners made a deal to sell the club to wealthy Edward J. DeBartolo of Youngstown, Ohio.

While I was sad to see Veeck leaving, I was delighted to see someone like DeBartolo coming in. He seemed to me to be the perfect owner for the 1980's.

He intended to keep the team in Chicago. And he was conservatively estimated to be worth $600 million.

I figured if he was willing to part with just a few of those $600 million to invest in baseball players, the woebegone White Sox, my favorite baseball team at the time, would get well and be competitive in a hurry. This was a man who could sit at the table all night with Steinbrenner, Autry, Turner, and Busch, and see every raise.

I became excited about the future.

But I was a little premature.

The owners of the other franchises in the American League let it be known, through Bowie K. Kuhn, that they would not approve Mr. DeBartolo's application for membership in their exclusive little club.

They gave two explanations for this:

Mr. DeBartolo owned racetracks. This, of course, did not stand up under even mild scrutiny, for two members of the club of baseball owners at the time, George Steinbrenner of the New York Yankees and John Galbreath of the Pittsburgh Pirates, also owned racetracks.

Mr. DeBartolo lived in Youngstown, had no intention of relocating, and would therefore be undesirable as an absentee owner. This also was a lot of crap. Or hadn't they noticed that Steinbrenner lived in Florida, and the fellow who owned the Seattle team lived in southern California, and the fellow who owned the Houston team lived in New Jersey?

Anyway, as the deal was falling apart, it was obvious that the owners didn't want DeBartolo in their exclusive fraternity for one reason or another. Perhaps because his name ended in a vowel. Perhaps because of all his money. Some of the other owners had to be worried that DeBartolo might make the White Sox *too* competitive.

So it was that a short time later, the White Sox were sold to a syndicate headed by Jerry Reinsdorf and Eddie Einhorn.

All I knew about them was that they were young, rich, and enthusiastic. I later learned that they had met at Northwestern Law School and shared an interest in sports. They had maintained their friendship over the years. Reinsdorf made a fortune syndicating real-estate deals through Balcor, the company he founded and later sold to American Express for $50 million. Einhorn had prospered by syndicating sports events through TVS, the company he founded and later sold to Dunn and Bradstreet for more than $5 million.

Reinsdorf and Einhorn might not have been in the financial bracket with DeBartolo, but they seemed pretty impressive—two self-made millionaires who had worked hard and long and set themselves up so they could finally indulge in their grand fantasy of owning and operating a major-league baseball team.

That sounded fine to me, but I decided to adopt a wait-and-see attitude.

I didn't have to wait too long. One of the first things they did after buying the team was to offer me a three-year contract. Einhorn, to his credit, understood television and knew that I had done pretty well by the club during my decade in Chicago.

I told them I wouldn't accept a three-year contract. They figured I was negotiating, looking for a better deal. And I told them that wasn't the case at all. I gave them the speech I was getting used to giving. The Charlie Finley speech:

"I don't know you fellows, you don't know me. I've been around a long time, and I know that things don't always work out the way you think they will. If we're happy, we can go on forever, but if we're not, I want to have a way out. So let's just go with a one-year contract and see how things work out."

When they realized I was adamant, they relented and agreed to the one-year deal.

And not quite twelve months later, I was delighted, because things didn't work out that well.

Nineteen eighty-one, all things considered, was not a very good year for Chicago White Sox baseball.

The principal problem was the strike.

Then, when the season resumed, the owners briefly suspended Jimmy Piersall, without much reason, I thought.

They thoroughly embarrassed and humiliated him in public, and altogether treated him shabbily. It seemed that club management was appalled that Piersall had used the expression "horny broads." Jimmy did this when he and I appeared on a television talk show hosted by *Tribune* columnist Mike Royko.

Here's exactly the way it happened.

Royko directed a question to me.

"Harry," he said, "I imagine one of the tough things about being an announcer is that wives and girlfriends listen to the broadcasts and take things out of context. Not being that familiar with the game, I bet they get offended. Or worse, tell their husbands or boyfriends things you said—or they *thought* you said."

"Exactly right," I replied. "Whether it's a wife or a girlfriend or a wife-to-be, they want to show an interest in their man's career, but they don't realize sometimes they can hurt rather than help. It's a problem."

That's when Jimmy cut in.

"Yeah, yeah," he said. "There are a lot of horny broads on the circuit."

Jimmy did not mean to offend. But White Sox management decided it was a slur against the wives of their ballplayers.

Now I've been in broadcasting a long time. I know what happens when something offensive goes out over the air. The switchboard lights up and the phones go crazy.

Nothing happened after Jimmy's innocent comment. Nothing at all.

The show was televised on a Saturday night. There were no calls on Saturday. No calls on Sunday. None on Monday or Tuesday. Wednesday, on Wally Phillips's morning radio show, Tony LaRussa was a guest.

Wally asked a general, easygoing question like, "How's everything going, Tony?"

And Tony replied, "Well, our wives are a little upset. They didn't take kindly to Jimmy Piersall calling them 'horny broads.' "

Thus began the controversy.

It was clearly a battle Jimmy couldn't win. They just wanted to get rid of him.

I didn't think anything of his choice of words. Neither did Royko; Veeck wouldn't have, either. But with the new White Sox owners, that phrase was a hanging offense, and they left him out there, twisting in the breeze, for everyone to see. The contrast between the way they handled Jimmy and the way Veeck had treated him was stark and telling.

A few days after the last game of the eventful 1981 season, Reinsdorf sent a letter to my attorneys, Saul Foos and Jeffrey Jacobs, saying they intended to renew my contract and that in due time they would be ready to negotiate.

And in due time, the negotiations got started when Reinsdorf and I agreed to meet for lunch one afternoon at the Barclay Club.

The first thing he wanted to talk about was my "philosophy of broadcasting." Now I was thinking to myself, What does this guy know about the philosophy of broadcasting? But I was nice and polite and I gave him an answer.

I told him, as I've told many people, that I'm a representative of the fan. I explained that I don't feel as if I work for the owner, the player, or the manager. I told him that the guy who hires and fires me is really the fan. My duty to the fan is to explain what happens on the field as honestly and as well as I can. I assured Reinsdorf that never in my life have I gone to a ballpark with the intention of being critical, but that sometimes when you explain what happens on the field it sounds critical. If a ballplayer's made an error, I cannot say he made a great play. And if he's struck out with the bases loaded, I cannot say he hit a home run.

I think he got my drift.

So then the second subject he raised was Tony LaRussa.

"Harry," he interjected, "a big thing is that we want you to help us make Tony LaRussa popular. He's not popular, and he thinks that you and Jimmy are the reason. He thinks you're too critical of him."

"That's ridiculous," I said. "All Tony LaRussa has to do to become the most popular man in town is win. But I can't help him win just like I can't make him lose. That's something *he's* got to face."

Then Reinsdorf told me again that LaRussa had been complaining about me. I asked when he had complained. And Reinsdorf said all year long.

"Even in September?" I asked.

"Yeah, always," Reinsdorf said. "I just left Tony in my office, and he brought it up again."

When I heard that, I really got burned up.

"Listen," I said, "if we do come to terms this year, it's going to be on one condition. That you and LaRussa and I go into a room by ourselves, because I've got to find out whether you're a liar or he's a liar."

Reinsdorf was surprised when he heard that. I have to admit I would have been, too, if I were he. But I explained to him why I was so furious.

All through September, LaRussa had been pulling me off to the side during batting practice or when we were traveling to compliment me, to tell me how great my broadcasts were. He told me that he had never really had a chance to hear me before, but since the club had started using a VCR to study game tapes, he'd been listening to my comments, too, and was impressed. At last, or so he said, he understood why I was so popular with the fans. It actually became pretty embarrassing, because if LaRussa praised me once, he praised me five or six times.

Reinsdorf was shocked to hear this story. He promised that he would get the matter resolved.

The next time Reinsdorf and I met, Einhorn was there, along with my attorneys. One thing I liked about Eddie—you knew where he was coming from, even if you didn't always agree with him. Anyway, at this meeting, Reinsdorf and Einhorn unveiled their plans for SportsVision, their bold new step into the future.

SportsVision was going to be an over-the-air pay-television outlet devoted exclusively to sports. The White Sox were going to be the main attraction, but Bulls basketball, Blackhawks hockey, and Sting soccer would also be televised, along with some boxing and tennis. Customers were going to be charged a one-time $50 installation fee, and $21.95 a month for the service. Reinsdorf and Einhorn were figuring on a windfall.

I asked one question.

"Are the people going to get the Cubs?"

"Hell, no," Einhorn said.

"Then, Eddie, it's not going to work," I said, prophetically.

"It's going to work," Einhorn insisted. "We're going to sell fifty thousand homes the first year. Once we do that, we're in the black. Lord knows how many millions we're going to make out of this."

I repeated that it wasn't going to work without the Cubs. It was simple and infallible logic.

"The Chicago Cubs are on free TV, on Channel Nine," I explained. "They televise a hundred-fifty games a year. Then, on Saturdays, NBC televises another twenty or thirty games a year for free. On Monday nights, you've got ABC televising another twelve or so free games each season. Now if I'm not mistaken, that means you have about two hundred free baseball games in this market. Do you think people are going to pay all that money for SportsVision when they can see over two hundred games for free? Why in the hell are they ever going to watch the White Sox again?"

They were surprised that I hadn't responded more positively to their sales pitch. In fact, Einhorn said, "I've made a fortune out of television sports. Who the hell are you to tell me what will or won't work?"

Well, it was clear our negotiations weren't going to go any further that day, so we agreed to meet a third time.

When I arrived for that third meeting, it was Einhorn and Reinsdorf again, and I was accompanied by Foos and Jacobs.

I had given a lot of thought to their SportsVision plan, and reiterated that I didn't think it could work without the Cubs. But I said I'd go along with them on one condition: I needed some security. After one year on SportsVision with no one watching, people might be saying, "Harry Who?" I explained to them the principle of out of sight, out of mind. So, the security, the insurance I wanted, was a three-to-five-year deal at the large numbers we were talking about.

They were shocked. They weren't prepared for that at all.

They said they were expecting to make a one-year deal just as they had the previous season—and they threw my usual arguments back in my face. I became suspicious. I got the distinct impression that their plan was to hire me for a year, use me to sell those fifty thousand customers, and then release me. A year ago, they were desperate to sign me for three years; now they wanted no part of it.

We were getting nowhere, so we decided to end the meeting. This was a Thursday. We would try to conclude the deal when we met again the following Tuesday.

But when I went home, I realized that the whole thing just didn't feel right. I gave some more thought to the Chicago Cubs. And the more I thought about them, the better they sounded.

The White Sox were talking about fifty thousand homes. The Cubs, meanwhile, were already seen in 28 *million* homes. Their games were carried over the Chicago superstation, WGN, which, like the ball club, was owned by the *Tribune*. And the Cubs were seen in every one of those 28 million homes for free. Moreover, Jack Brickhouse had retired at the end of the 1981 season, and the Cubs were in the market for a new announcer.

To be truthful, after Brickhouse left and after Dallas Green came in to run the club, I fully expected the Cubs to contact me. But they didn't. So, after fifteen minutes or a half hour of giving all these facts serious consideration, I picked up the telephone and called Andy McKenna.

Andy, who had been involved with Bill Veeck's group when it owned the White Sox, was now chairman of the Cubs' board.

"Andy," I kidded on the square, "to be honest with you, I'm very disappointed that your people haven't contacted me. But you didn't call me, so now I'm calling you. I have a very substantial one-year offer to return to the White Sox, and I have to make a decision by Tuesday. But before I make a decision, I wanted to know for sure what the Cubs think. Is there any chance that you're interested in me doing the Cubs games?"

Andy paused.

"Do you have any commitments, any options, any understandings, any promises with any other team?" he asked.

"No, I've been a free agent since the end of the season."

"Let me call you back within ten minutes," he said.

It wasn't five minutes later when the phone rang again.

"Yes, we're interested," McKenna said. "You're going to get a phone call from Jim Dowdle, the head of Continental Broadcasting. He'll take it from here."

Continental Broadcasting is the division of the Tribune Company that operates WGN and the other radio and television stations the company owns.

Sure enough, a few minutes later, Dowdle called, and within a half hour he was sitting in my apartment at the Ambassador East, talking about my future with the Chicago Cubs.

Dowdle doesn't drink, he doesn't talk in circles. He was just there to do business. Dowdle wanted to know why I wanted to move to the Cubs. I told him honestly about my reservations about SportsVision, Reinsdorf, and Einhorn.

"I want to pursue this," he said. "But we don't have much time. There are a few other people I want you to talk to."

I told him I was at his disposal.

But there was one problem. I was too damn visible. I just couldn't be seen talking to all the Cubs' officials days before I was supposed to re-sign with the White Sox.

Finally, Dowdle came up with a quiet place—the Chicago Club. He gave me the address, and I agreed to meet the next day. He told me to go into the lobby, not even *look* at anybody, and head right for the meeting room.

But the minute I stepped into the lobby, it was a lot of, "Hey, Harry! How ya doin'?" or "Harry, who ya seein' here?"

Not as secret as I would have hoped.

Anyway, I met again with Jim Dowdle and McKenna—plus Dallas Green, the general manager of the Cubs, plus Stanton Cook and John Madigan, the two top executives for the Tribune Company. By Saturday, we had a deal. By Sunday, we had contracts written out in longhand on yellow legal pads. And we decided to hold a press conference on Monday.

On Monday morning, I realized I'd better let Reinsdorf and Einhorn know that something was up. They were at opposite ends of town, so we got together on a conference call.

I told them we could cancel the meeting we had scheduled for Tuesday, that it wouldn't be necessary. They wanted to know if I was going someplace else, and I just responded that I wasn't going to be returning to the White Sox. Reinsdorf reminded me that they had made me a substantial offer—and they had—and that I was leaving on my own, I wasn't being fired. I understood that, I assured him. There wouldn't be any problem at all as long as they didn't start popping off in the newspapers. I thanked them, wished them well, and hung up.

Then I went downstairs, where the Chicago Cubs and WGN were about to hold a joint press conference announcing that Harry Caray would be joining their broadcast team as the number-one play-by-play announcer for the 1982 season.

Which only turned out to be the best move I'd made in my career since I wrote that letter to Merle Jones.

WGN, the Chicago Cubs' superstation, is now in about 30 million homes equipped with cable television.

And SportsVision was a flop. They still haven't sold it to fifty thousand subscribers.

RUNS HITS CHAPTER

0 0 18

"A REAL (DUTCH) TREAT"

The 1988 season with the Cubs provided many memories for me, not the least of which was the fact that it marked my first full year back in the booth after my stroke.

Quite obviously, I was a lot stronger than during the 1987 season. I resumed my regular routine, business as usual—off to Mesa, Arizona, for spring training in March, then to Atlanta for Opening Day, then on through until October 2, our last game at Wrigley Field against the Pittsburgh Pirates. I didn't miss an inning, and I felt great.

As I said earlier, I felt pretty good when I came back in 1987, but I will admit that I mispronounced a few words and botched a few names along the way. Upon returning, I was more conscious of these mistakes, thinking it was the stroke that caused them. Gradually, I realized that it was no big deal. People who've had strokes told me that this is a common thing, that it takes a while before you become perfect again. Not that I was ever perfect in the first place. I've been known to botch a word or two on the air during the best of times.

I didn't let these occasional mistakes bother me, and apparently, they weren't disturbing my superiors or my listeners. The fan mail I got during 1988 led me to believe that the audience was happy to have me back for 162 games. I know I certainly was happy.

I wish the Cubs could have finished first instead of fourth, but there were many highlights. And if you can't broadcast for a pennant winner, I suppose what happened on September 30 at Wrigley Field is a pretty good substitute. It was a Friday-afternoon game, the first of our last homestand against the Pirates. I had no idea what was on tap that day when I woke up at the Ambassador East Hotel downtown, had my breakfast, and read the papers as I always did. I thought it would be a cool day, so I dressed in a jacket and tie. Good thing I wore the tie, as it turned out.

When I got to Wrigley Field, I went downstairs to the field level to tape the pregame show with manager Don Zimmer. Then I went upstairs and noticed that there were all these drapes over the railing that hangs over the stands below. I went into the booth and began unpacking my briefcase when I saw Bill Lotzer, an executive of WGN-TV who you don't see around the ballpark very much—at least not at that early hour.

"What's going on around here, Bill?" I said. "Why all those drapes outside?"

He didn't answer me. He just took off. Then, five minutes later, he returned.

"You asked me a question a while ago, but I couldn't answer you until I cleared it," he said. "Keep this to yourself, but we're expecting President Reagan here today. He's in Chicago today, and we think he's coming to the ballpark."

"President Reagan!" I practically shouted. "Great."

As time went on, I learned that he was not only going to come to the ballpark, but that he was insisting on coming upstairs to the broadcast booth. As I understood it, the Secret Service detail that always travels with him was trying desperately to talk him out of it. But, no, President Ronald Reagan, with all this pressure on him and all these people following him around—security personnel, reporters, cameras—wanted to come up to the booth, where he had done play-by-play many years ago. I thought to myself, Here's the most powerful man in the world and he wants to escape for a half hour, to recapture his youth, to do something he wanted to do just for the sake of doing it. I thought it was great.

Little did I know that my wife, Dutchie, had a clue about all this excitement before I did. Jim Dowdle of Continental Broadcasting had called the hotel after I'd left and asked her if she was planning to go to the ballpark that day. Dutchie said no, she had other things to do. Dowdle suggested that it might be a game she wouldn't want to miss, and Dutchie figured it out. She'd seen on TV that morning that the president was in town and she knows he's a baseball fan. She showered in a hurry and headed for Wrigley Field, long after the biggest dog you'll ever want to see came into our booth sniffing around while I was filling out the lineup card. Another security measure, of which there were many.

When Steve Stone and I came on the air at our usual time, I didn't say right away that the president would be at the ballpark any minute. I just sort of hinted around it, kidding with Steve that we had a big surprise for everybody. Steve asked if I could provide any clues. Well, I said, I can tell you this. He used to broadcast Cub games a long time ago, but since has gone on to bigger and better. I suspect that the viewers got the idea then. Meanwhile, the game was being delayed slightly and the fans in Wrigley Field didn't have to have a wild sense of imagination to realize that something highly unusual was pending. It isn't every day that you see sharpshooters on the rooftops of nearby buildings and on the top of the ballpark itself. There was a lot of milling around on the field too.

Pretty soon, this huge motorcade rolled toward the Wrigley Field entrance and President Reagan was escorted into the Cubs' locker room, which had been vacated. As I was told later, he spent a few minutes down there actually warming up. He had agreed to throw out the opening pitch, and he was seeing if he could do it comfortably enough while wearing a bulletproof vest. The security detail wasn't going to allow him on the field without that. No way.

Finally, there was all this commotion around the tunnel that leads from the Cubs' clubhouse to their dugout, where all the Cub players were waiting expectantly, a few of them with cameras. At last, here came the procession of security people and then, all dressed up in a shiny blue Cubs' jacket, the president of the United States. Well, I've been around a long time and I've seen a lot of politicians and movie stars and former athletes introduced before ball games, but when the public-address announcer informed the fans at Wrigley Field that afternoon that they'd been waiting patiently for some twenty or thirty minutes because President Reagan was there to throw out the first ball . . . well, he got a tremendous ovation. A warm, warm welcome. He received a terrific round of applause when he first showed up, another when he went to the mound, then another when he disappeared back into the Cubs' clubhouse.

And then it was time for him to come upstairs to do some

play-by-play. The president was a little out of breath when he first showed up. Remember, there are no elevators or escalators at Wrigley Field. All of us who climb from the field level to press level do it by walking a long ramp, so I could understand why Mr. Reagan needed a moment to catch his breath. Steve and I welcomed him and told him that whenever he felt like taking it away, that was fine with us. And when that time came, I thought the president was terrific. You could tell by the way he described the game before him that he'd done it before and done it well. I tried to stay out of the way as much as possible, filling in a pitch here and there or describing a replay.

Otherwise, President Reagan did an outstanding job, and he had some pretty good lines too.

"I'll be out of work in a couple months," he said, "so I thought I might come up here and audition."

After a couple of innings, one of his aides wrote me a note that Mr. Reagan would have to go. I prevailed upon him to stay until after the commercial break so we could thank him and say good-bye. I also threw in a line of my own, after complimenting him on a very fine job.

"Mr. Reagan," I said. "You'd be a great anchorman on the evening news. At least it would give you a chance to get even."

And off he went, along with all those Secret Service agents and all those reporters. Mr. Reagan looked terrific and I said so on the air. For all the stress a president endures, I was amazed. Mr. Reagan is a personable and handsome man—a few flecks of gray in his air, but very young and very vibrant-looking. The pictures of him broadcasting the Cub game that day went all over the country—on TV, in newspapers. I couldn't help marveling at how remarkable it was that Mr. Reagan—the *president of the United States*—had broadcast with me not once but *twice* in his incredible career. It was a very special day for Harry Caray, who just happened to be wearing a jacket and tie.

If September 30 was the red-letter day of 1988, the evening of August 8 wasn't far behind. That was the occasion of the first night game in the history of Wrigley Field—Cubs vs. Philadelphia Phillies, a real event, even if it was postponed because of rain after a long, long delay in the fourth inning. It had been a nice, warm day, the ball game started with all the fanfare, and then, boom, this tremendous storm hit Wrigley Field. So the first official night game wasn't really played until the next night, August 9, against the New York Mets. A lot of people suggested that this was God's way of saying that lights didn't belong at Wrigley Field, but I really think that He has more important things to worry about. I don't think the Good Lord had any effect on August 8.

I will say that I was never a great proponent of night baseball at Wrigley Field, and I'm still not. Having said that, though, let me remind everybody that the Cubs and the Tribune Company were forced to install lights. The commissioner of baseball, Peter Ueberroth, stated in 1984, when the Cubs won the division and entered the playoffs, that if the Cubs were to participate in the postseason again, they would have to play their games in another ballpark—St. Louis or Pittsburgh—a ballpark with lights, a ballpark that could host night games, for the benefit of network television and prime-time revenues. So the Cubs organization didn't bring about August 8, 1988, out of greed. It was out of need.

Now, the Cubs played six night games during 1988 (besides the rainout), with interesting results. The attendance figures gradually went down, which might have been because the weather was getting colder and because the team wasn't contending. Also, there were about ten other games that started during daylight hours but were finished with the lights on. The lights really help there, when you have a 3 P.M. start under an overcast sky. Or a 3 P.M. start for a ball game that goes into extra innings.

I also noticed that I heard more booing of Cub players during six night games than I heard during eight years of broadcasting Cub day games. I don't know how you conduct a study on the whys and wherefores of that, but I know it was there. I suspect that during day games people have a more happy-go-lucky, care-free attitude. It's like a picnic. You're out in the fresh air, you have a couple beers, you get some sunshine, you look at the pretty girls, whatever. It's a pleasant, fun atmosphere at a beautiful ballpark. Of course, you want the Cubs to win, but if they don't, well, it's not the end of the world. You've still had a good time.

But when you have a night game, you're not selling sunshine and ivy. The viewer is more cynical, more critical—maybe because he or she has had a tough day at the office, maybe because he is there to watch a baseball game, period. He's not there to get a tan. At a night game, the expectation of the fan is higher. More focused. He's not out there for a picnic, he's out there to see the product on the field. And when he doesn't see the Cubs win, he's more conscious of the fact that maybe he didn't get his money's worth.

I think the players had better realize that they're going to be playing to a different audience at night. They're going to be judged differently, and in the end, it might be better for the ball club. Better for the franchise. I'm not saying that the Cubs exist in a country-club atmosphere, but I do say that crowds at night games will be a little harder in their appraisals. It won't matter as much whether a player is popular or good-looking to the night audience. The night audience is going to want results. When a guy can't do the job, the fan's only recourse is to boo. The typical daytime Cub fan still would be happy to see Randy Hundley catching, Phil Cavarretta at first, Ryne Sandberg at second, Ernie Banks at shortstop, Billy Williams in the outfield . . . and so on. If Cub players played until they were a hundred years old, it wouldn't matter.

But that will change with night games, I think. One of the reasons why the Cubs haven't been more successful might be the fact that fans have been content for so many years to go to this beautiful ballpark on a beautiful summer afternoon . . . and if the Cubs happen to win, great. That's a bonus. Winning isn't the name of the game. If they do, fine. But if they don't, well, let's go back tomorrow. Now, though, players who have become heroes very easily with the Cubs might not become heroes so easily with the lights on.

I think of the fans more than the players, and I think what the Cubs have going now is just about right. There are a lot of people who work during the days and can't get away to watch a game. For them, night games are a blessing. As long as the Cubs don't play any more than eighteen night games a season, that's fine with me. There still will be so many more day games that the Cubs and Wrigley Field won't lose that mystique, that uniqueness. I accept the word of the Tribune Company, which says that the limit will be eighteen. I also know that history indicates a few night games can turn into a few more and a few more. Once eighteen becomes nineteen, it'll be the beginning of the end.

As a kid, all I thought about was baseball, and the fact that I could go to a ball game during the day increased my interest and love of the sport. The Cubs have generations of fans who grew up watching the team. If the Cubs started playing a lot of night games, would that continue? I doubt it. You know, throughout the major leagues, teams hire merchandising and marketing experts for one reason—to get young people interested in the game, to cultivate new fans. And the Cubs have this built into the franchise. Every major league baseball team would give anything to have what the Cubs have, but the Cubs were forced to make an adjustment. If the Cubs remain adamant about having just eighteen night games, they can have the best of both worlds.

Another unusual thing struck me that first night at Wrigley Field. A lot of residents had been worried about the effect of having all these cars and fans around after dark, but that neighborhood has to be one of the safest places in Chicago when the Cubs are playing at night. Those lights not only illuminate the field, they illuminate the streets and sidewalks. Plus, there are all those added police officers around for a night game. I would venture to guess that the homeowners around Wrigley Field who were concerned about vandalism or noise or whatever were pleasantly surprised by how smoothly things went. There might have been some parking problems, but they have parking problems for day games too.

Besides the night games, 1988 marked the debut of the Jim Frey era as general manager of the Cubs. He was the manager when the Cubs won the National League East title in 1984, but was fired in 1986 by Dallas Green. The next year, Frey came on as an analyst on our WGN radio broadcasts. Then, in one of the peculiar twists of fate that you see in life as well as sports, Frey was hired to replace Green, who resigned under pressure.

The Cubs of 1988 had a lineup featuring some terrific young and promising players, such as Mark Grace, Rafael Palmeiro, Mark Grace, Damon Berryhill. Grace started the season in the minors, but you could see in spring training that this kid was a natural. When Frey traded Leon Durham to Cincinnati early in the season, the Cubs immediately put Grace at first base, where he'll probably play for the next ten or fifteen years. Palmeiro, the left fielder, was up among the league's leading hitters all season. Critics contend that he didn't knock in enough runs, but I think he's going to be terrific. This statistic about "game-winning RBI" is one of the phoniest in baseball, anyway. Can you imagine, if you bat in your team's first run to give your team a 1–0 lead, and your team doesn't relinquish the lead and goes on to win the game 10–9, you get a "game-winning RBI"? Now, that's ridiculous. What does it mean?

Greg Maddux, an outstanding right-handed pitcher, won fifteen games by the All-Star break and was the ace of the staff. Berryhill did such a good job of catching that veteran Jody Davis was traded to the Atlanta Braves just before the season ended. Add those youngsters to a shortstop like Shawon Dunston, who really matured; to Ryne Sandberg, who is still *the* second baseman in the National League; to Vance Law, a free agent who became the Cubs' best third baseman since Ron Santo in his palmiest days; and to Andre Dawson, one of the best all-around players in either league. You've got a pretty good lineup there, a better lineup than the one the Los Angeles Dodgers put out every day, and the Dodgers won the World Series.

What the Dodgers had—in addition to a great manager, Tommy Lasorda—was pitching, and that's exactly what the Cubs need. The Cubs will be whistling in the dark if they don't improve their pitching for 1989. Frey made a move early in his tenure that could be second-guessed. During the winter before the 1988 season, he dealt Lee Smith, the Cubs' best relief pitcher for several years, to the Boston Red Sox for Calvin Schiraldi and Al Nipper. I don't so much fault Frey for trading Smith. I fault him for not shopping Smith around. I believe Frey could have gotten more in return for Smith and I believe Frey would tell you the same thing today if you asked him. Heck, Lasorda told me that the Dodgers would have given the Cubs Bob Welch and somebody else in return for Smith, but the Dodgers didn't think Smith was available. So the Dodgers sent Welch to Oakland, where he won seventeen games and lost only nine for the American League Champion Athletics. With all the teams in search of a hard-throwing relief pitcher, you just wish Frey had tested the waters a bit more.

But you have to give Frey credit for getting Law from the Montreal Expos and for going with the kids. You also have to give Frey credit for hiring Zimmer, who did a fine job as manager. There was a lot of criticism at the outset, because some people thought Frey and Zimmer, who have known each other since high school, were too close. Well, the relationship didn't hurt a bit. A general manager and a field manager should be close. During Green's reign, it was embarrassing to see how he treated Gene Michael, who replaced Frey. At the end of Frey's term, it was embarrassing to see how Green treated him, and here was a guy who had managed the team to first place for the first time since 1945! Frey would try to advance his own personal opinions, but they weren't accepted.

Still, Dallas Green was a good general manager for the Cubs. He took over in 1981 when the Tribune Company bought the team from the Wrigley family, and three years later, the Cubs won ninety-six games. There was a certain spontaneity about Dallas. When he saw the team needed something, he tried to get it and usually did. He brought over Keith Moreland and Sandberg from Philadelphia, where Dallas had won the World Series as manager of the Phillies in 1980. Then he traded for Gary Matthews and Bob Dernier just before the 1984 regular season. Then, when he saw that the Cubs had a chance to finish first, he went out and got Rick Sutcliffe from Cleveland and Dennis Eckersley from Boston. Sutcliffe went 16-1 for the Cubs and won the Cy Young Award.

Where Dallas Green changed is when he became president of the ball club too. He started thinking differently. All of a sudden, he was surrounded by four or five people who were helping to make decisions for him. That wasn't the Dallas Green we knew at the start. The man we knew was somebody who had a notion and then said, boom, let's do it. But when Dallas was elevated beyond the level of his competency—the old Peter Principle—when he became surrounded by a committee of experts, it was all different. Dallas Green, the outstanding general manager, wasn't just a general manager anymore. He was trying to do everything when he should have been just worrying about putting the ball club on the field.

For that 1984 season, you'll recall, the Cubs had brought in Jim Finks as president. Finks is an experienced executive with a wide background in sports. He'd been general manager of the Bears before, and is general manager of the New Orleans Saints now. With the Cubs, Finks handled a lot of administrative work and left Dallas to build a ball club. I don't know how Dallas and Finks got along, but if Dallas doesn't realize what a plus it was for him having Finks around, I'd be disappointed. It's when Dallas took on all those responsibilities that he ceased being the effective general manager he was at the outset.

Dallas Green deserves some credit for all these kids we see on the field for the Cubs now. But let's look around baseball. Every team has some young players in the lineup. If your farm system doesn't produce four players in eight years, something's seriously wrong. You should get more than four players in that time. The farm system has to come up with something. Not only that, but in 1983 the Cubs could have drafted Roger Clemens, the star pitcher of the Boston Red Sox. Who did the Cubs select? Jackie Davidson, who had a sore arm when he graduated from high school. In 1984, the Cubs took Drew Hall. They could have had Cory Snyder, a star with the Cleveland Indians, or Mark McGwire, a slugger for the Oakland Athletics. How can you not draft a power hitter like that when you play eighty-one games in Wrigley Field?

You could make a heck of a case against the Dallas Green regime on that basis, but I still think he was a good general manager. I don't know about his scouts or his farm system. You would think a ball club would get more than the Cubs got through their development program. Do you fault Dallas for that, or the people below him? I suppose he had to take some of the blame. Just as he had to take some of the blame for firing all those managers he hired. Just as you have to wonder why he paid guys like Moreland $1.5 million—creating a situation inherited by Frey, who not only wanted to dump some salaries but the players who were getting them. I don't know how any ballplayer could be mad at Dallas Green—not after the way he paid them. At the end of the 1987 season, he got angry at a few of them, and called some of them "quitters." Well, it was some of those "quitters" he overpaid who got him out of Chicago. Now, he's in New York as manager of George Steinbrenner's Yankees. At least he was when this book went to press.

I'm concerned about the Cubs, though, and how they're going to improve their pitching. The Dodgers proved during the World Series what we've been saying forever, that pitching is at least 75 percent of baseball. The Cubs have to be careful about not breaking up that young nucleus of theirs. Yet, even if Grace and Berryhill and Dunston improve as you expect they will, the Cubs of 1989 will wind up just where they wound up in 1988 unless they get better pitching. I marvel at what the Dodgers did, yet it didn't really surprise me because they had the arms and they had Lasorda. He's always been a great goodwill ambassador. He's always talking so much about his great appetite for pasta and his many friends in Hollywood like Frank Sinatra. Sometimes all of these other things Lasorda does make you forget that he's been a great manager too. Look at his record.

But 1988 was good to me too. I was back doing what I love to do, broadcasting baseball with people like Steve Stone, who's like a son to me, Dewayne Staats, and Davey Nelson. Believe me, I've been in situations where you dread going into the booth because you have to work with a guy you don't particularly enjoy. There's none of that with the Cubs, even when Steve is wielding one of those rotten cigars of his. The year also marked the first anniversary of my restaurant, Harry Caray's, in downtown Chicago. In November, I went to Las Vegas for a roast in my honor at Bally's Casino-Resort. And then on to Palm Springs, my winter home, where I made myself a promise to take up golf again. I used to play many years ago, but I was the original terrible-tempered Tommy Bott, screaming and throwing clubs and getting angry. The game was ruining my disposition. So I quit cold turkey, even though I could shoot a respectable score. Well, now I live right on the sixth hole at the beautiful Canyon Country Club in Palm Springs. They say age mellows all of us, so I'll try again.

Still, I'm a lot like Lasorda. He's always said the saddest day of the year is the day the baseball season ends, and I have to agree with him. I've cut back on my broadcasting load in recent years. I don't do the other sports I used to do anymore because I don't need the money. I only do baseball. And I don't do baseball because I need the money. I do it because I need baseball. I love baseball. I'm an enthusiastic guy. I'll talk to you all night about politics or the economy or foreign policy, but what I most enjoy talking about is baseball.

That's my living, that's my life, and I thank God for it. At my age, after all these years, I still love going to the ballpark. Every day is a new challenge. You'll never see two ball games alike, never two plays alike. You forget the scores, but not the people. And that's why, as soon as today's game is overwith, I can't wait until tomorrow's game. I've thought about taking a day off once in a while during the season, but where would I rather be than the ballpark? And if I wasn't there one day, that's probably just the day I'd miss something.

I am, after all, a fan.

ABOUT THE AUTHORS

HARRY CARAY, one of the most unique sportscasters in history, will be entering his forty-sixth consecutive season of baseball play-by-play broadcasting in 1989. He was the voice of the St. Louis Cardinals for a quarter century, before joining the Oakland A's for one season and the Chicago White Sox for eleven. He has been the TV and radio voice of the Chicago Cubs since 1982.

BOB VERDI is the syndicated sports columnist for the *Chicago Tribune*. His previous books are *McMahon!*, the best-selling autobiography of Chicago Bears quarterback Jim McMahon, and *The Bob Verdi Collection*, a sampling of his columns.